Internship Guide

Latest 71.

Internship Guide

Work Placements Step by Step

Esther Haag

eleven
international publishing

Published, sold and distributed by Eleven International Publishing
P.O. Box 85576
2508 CG The Hague
The Netherlands
Tel.: +31 70 33 070 33
Fax: +31 70 33 070 30
e-mail: sales@budh.nl
www.elevenpub.com

Sold and distributed in USA and Canada
International Specialized Book Services
920 NE 58th Avenue, Suite 300
Portland, OR 97213-3786, USA
Tel: 1-800-944-6190 (toll-free)
Fax: +1 503 280-8832
orders@isbs.com
www.isbs.com

Eleven International Publishing is an imprint of Boom uitgevers Den Haag.

Photographer: Elmer Spaargaren
Cover photograph and photograph p. 162: Albert Everaarts

ISBN 978-94-90947-88-0
ISBN 978-94-6094-675-2 (e-book)
© 2013 Esther Haag | Eleven International Publishing

Printed in The Netherlands

www.internshipguide.elevenpub.com

Preface

Whether you want to do a placement at home or abroad, this book provides practically all the information you need when looking for and arranging your placement.[1]

I sincerely thank all students who have contributed to this book by asking me their questions. I would also like to thank all the people who inspired me to write this book: careers advisors, colleagues, tennis buddies, my family and friends. I am grateful to Jacqueline van Kruiningen for her confidence and her detailed feedback on the first draft of the manuscript, and I owe a heartfelt 'thank you' to my children for their support and their lovely book covers. I also want to thank Bryn van Helden and Cees Krottje for this translation and Julia Gonzalez, Robert Wagenaar and Richard de Lavigne for their contribution.

Esther Haag
Haren, September 2012

---

[1]   A placement is sometimes referred to as an 'internship' or a 'traineeship'. This book chooses to use the term 'placement' (or 'work placement') in line with the European Committee, which also uses the word to indicate a practical period within a working environment as part of a degree programme at a higher educational institution.

Foreword

As joint coordinators of the Tuning projects, we are very pleased to add this *Internship Guide* to the range of publications that were developed in the framework of the Tuning initiative. Tuning Educational Structures in Europe was set up to implement the political objectives of the Bologna Process and the Lisbon Strategy at the level of higher education institutions. It has developed tools to implement student-centred, outcome-based and transparent higher educational programmes.

The shift to student-centred, outcome-based and transparent degree programmes in higher education is not limited to Europe. It fits into a worldwide process of educational reform and innovation to make degree programmes and 'qualifications' (academic awards or certification given on completion of a programme) 'fit *of* purpose' as well 'fit *for* purpose'. This means that the competences fostered in degree programmes should meet the needs and expectations of students and society, enhancing employability, personal development and citizenship as well as meeting academic standards.

To make this possible, links between higher education and society and the labour market are required. The Tuning approach fosters these links through various means, including organizing wide-scale consultations of stakeholders (students, graduates, employers and academics) on the importance of listed subject-specific as well as generic competences. The level of achievement of competences by students is expressed in learning outcomes, which are determined by the higher education institutions. This learning outcomes-competence based approach has been and is being widely adopted not only in Europe, but indeed throughout the world. It increases the compatibility and comparability of educational programmes for all stakeholders, including employers.

This *Internship Guide* fits very well in this process and is an essential complement to the work already done in the Tuning framework. It is fully in accord with the Tuning methodology (<www.unideusto.org/tuningeu/>), which is based on a step-by-step approach to enhance degree programmes and their course units. The Tuning methodology with competences and learning outcomes at its heart, so well reflected in this Internship Guide, guarantees that the placements contribute significantly to the level and thus the quality that the degree programme aims for. Work placements are a way for students to apply the competences achieved in their educational programme in practice in the labour market, and to further develop them and thus achieve the learning outcomes of their degree programme. The placement should be seen as an excellent example of the student-centred and active learning approach. Last but not least, including placements in the curriculum is a good means to stimulate national and international student mobility.

Although internships or (work) placements are increasingly becoming a component of higher education degree programmes, in many countries it is still a relatively new phenomena. A work placement differs from other degree programme components in that students are often required to look for a placement themselves. This and the fact that placements deal with a third party outside university makes it difficult for degree programme organizers to arrange this non-traditional type of subject into their curriculum.

The descriptions of the steps to arrange work placements in this *Internship Guide* are based specifically on twenty-five years of experience with placements in the curricula at the Faculty of Arts of the University of Groningen. Although small compared with other European countries, the Netherlands has built up a tradition with placements in higher education. Since the end of the 1980s, students at Dutch universities of applied sciences as well as at research universities have undertaken placements in a wide range of countries and organizations.

This book aims to provide guidance to both university staff and students in describing the steps they need to take to organize and find placements that meet the learning outcomes of the degree programme and give the student a framework to put into practice the competences they developed during their studies and to enhance them further on the labour market.

We hope the placements (your) students manage to find to complement their degree programmes will provide a learning experience that will prepare them better for participation in the labour market and society as a whole.

Julia Gonzalez (University of Deusto, Bilbao) and Robert Wagenaar (University of Groningen)
Joint coordinators of the *Tuning Educational Structures in the World* process and co-directors of the *Tuning International Academy*.

Table of Contents

12

Introduction

A growing number of students in higher education (research universities and universities of applied sciences) have the opportunity to put their knowledge into practice by means of a work placement. While the importance of placements is increasingly emphasized in education policy and teaching inspections, there is still a considerable lack of knowledge regarding placement procedures among placement coordinators, lecturers, and placement providers. After all, students have the world at their feet, and this is especially true of students on placement: so many organizations, so many placements. As long as the level and extent of the placement meet the requirements, virtually *anything* is possible.

For that reason, in every degree programme, a placement is a subject in itself. No other course component unit offers students so much freedom yet presents so many difficulties: freedom because placements, by definition, largely take place beyond the lecturer's reach; difficulties because placements are carried out completely unaided. You will be asked to complete your placement independently and to comply with the wishes of two different parties, and the requirements of your degree programme often differ considerably from those of your placement provider.

The only proper way of looking at a placement, therefore, is to consider it a project with you as project leader. It is a project with a learning objective, an assignment, and a plan. The project has two supervisors: the lecturer and the supervisor within the host organization. Only one of them, the lecturer (or the Board of Examiners of your degree programme), will assess your placement. It is emphasized that all placement projects that are not assessed by a lecturer, and are therefore not rewarded with credits, are beyond the scope of this book.

If we approach placements as projects, we can also organize them as such. The easiest thing to do is to divide the project into steps, which can then be taken one by one. A placement is no static entity; its organization requires flexibility, which is why the order of steps is not completely fixed. The reason for this is that the steps allow for a certain degree of interaction: after Step 3, the student might feel the need to return to Step 1, etc.

Naturally, the steps you take and the order in which you take them largely depend on your degree programme. This book allows you to easily select the steps that apply to your placement. It also functions as a reference guide; you can look up terms and definitions in the extensive index in the back. If you think terms or steps are missing, please let us know by visiting the website at <www.internshipguide. elevenpub.com>. This website also provides links to interesting sites as well as a teacher's guide.

This book is divided into the following placement steps; each chapter covers one step:
Step 1   Orientation
Step 2   Self-analysis
Step 3   Market analysis
Step 4   Networking
Step 5   Applying for a placement
Step 6   The interview
Step 7   The placement
Step 8   Rounding off your placement

Although this book constantly refers to 'the placement', it is useful to distinguish between the most common types of placement:
1. orientational placement: students are given an impression of an organization;
2. observational placement: students participate in ongoing activities and carry out tasks at the level of a junior employee;
3. practical placement: students apply knowledge and skills acquired in class to a project;
4. research placement: students carry out independent scientific research;
5. consultancy placement: students advise the organization in question about a complicated problem or about organizational policy.
    (*Source: Abma et al., 2008*)

All steps will, to a greater or lesser extent, feature in every type of placement. Which step you take at which moment largely depends on you. Some students find it easier to decide what kind of placement they want to do – and to find one – than others. The clearer your idea about what you want, the easier it will be to find it. Some students have to look for a placement themselves, while others are provided with one. One piece of advice: take your time to decide what kind of placement you would like to do, even if your university is going to help you find one! A placement provides a unique opportunity to catch a glimpse behind the scenes; putting some time and effort into it will be worth your while.

Step 1 Orientation

What do we understand by the term 'placement'? In all cases in this book, a placement is considered to be a course unit that carries credits. Periods of work undertaken during your time as a student that are not included in your list of grades or your degree certificate are not covered by this book, although they usually don't differ all that much. To distinguish between the two, we will call the latter 'volunteer work'.

Your placement might be a compulsory component of your degree programme, or perhaps you are given permission to include one as an exception. You will then try to find out whether a placement is still a possibility for you, and this will lead you directly to the most difficult step of the placement process: orientation.

Apart from gaining the necessary experience often required by employers, there are several other reasons why you might consider doing a placement. Here are some reasons that students have given:

1. You want to find out what options your degree programme has to offer (what is it exactly that I am learning? *E.g.* Communication Studies).
2. You want to find out if a particular profession appeals to you (would I enjoy it? *E.g.* teaching).
3. You want to find out if a particular professional field suits you (would I feel comfortable there? *E.g.* diplomacy).
4. You want to find out whether you are suitable for a particular profession (will I be able to do it? *E.g.* researcher).
5. You want to gain work experience in your own field.
6. You want to fill a gap in your knowledge.
7. You want to become acquainted with people in order to build up a network (possibly internationally).
8. You want to find out which follow-up programme might suit you.
9. You want to go abroad for a while in order to achieve one of the above-mentioned goals and to brush up on your language skills.

These and others are all legitimate reasons for undertaking a placement, but some reasons require more orientation than others. Example: for Reason 6, a placement is not necessarily the best option. In this case, you might want to opt for a part-time job rather than a placement because the latter requires two supervisors and is therefore more complex.

The idea of undertaking a placement usually does not just fall from the sky. Most students have already given it some thought earlier on in their studies. As soon as you start seriously considering the option, your *orientation* begins: the first step of the search process, and also the most difficult one. It is a period with many questions and only a few answers. Here are some questions you might have:

Orientation Questions
- I would like to do a placement, but how do I go about it?
- There is a placement I would like to do, but how do I know if I qualify?
- I would like to undertake a placement with a particular organization; what do I arrange with them?
- I would like to go on placement but I have a wide range of interests; how will I be able to choose?
- What types of placements are possible within the framework of my degree programme?
- What is the lecturer's role in arranging a placement assignment?
- What order of steps should I follow when arranging a placement?
- How long does a placement have to be, and is it possible to do a part-time placement?
- I want to go on placement, but I do want to get paid. What would be a reasonable remuneration?
- What is the minimum and maximum duration of a placement?
- How much work can you do in a three-month placement?
- Who will supervise me during my placement?

The problem with all these questions is that they all belong to different fields and often need to be answered by different people. Some questions relate to placement conditions, some questions are content-related, some are concerned with how your placement is organized, and some relate to your wishes and abilities. This phase is about literally (*i.e.* actively) *searching* for information.

1.1 Placement Criteria

The starting point of your search will probably be your course catalogue. Perhaps your faculty provides a placement coordinator to help you, or a student support service or placement office. You can go there with all your questions about the preconditions or *formal criteria* of your placement: matters such as the length of the placement, the period in which your placement should take place, the minimum number of days a week that must be spent on placement, the question whether or not you are allowed to go abroad, and, if so, whether you should apply for a placement grant (*e.g.* travel allowance), questions about insurance, taxes, etc. This information is often also provided on the university website or on the website of your degree programme; for instance in the digital learning environment or on the intranet. All these criteria will be discussed in more detail further on in this book.

1.1.1 Length

In practice, placements may vary considerably in length. Some orientational placements take only a few days, but the minimum length of a full placement is seven weeks. The maximum length of a placement is a year. In some cases, it is possible to combine a placement with a dissertation or thesis that together form a 'final-year project'. Placements that lend themselves to this are, for example, large-scale ones that have the character of a research project, or placements yielding information that merits further research in a thesis. In some cases you are specifically required to write a separate placement report, whereas other degree programmes do not allow for that.

1.1.2 Full-Time or Part-Time

It may sometimes be necessary to spread a full-time placement over a longer period, thus making it a part-time placement. The number of credits helps you calculate the number of weeks. Example: a 10-ECTS placement at a Dutch university equals 10×28 hours = 280 hours, which equals a full-time placement of seven weeks (40 hours per week). In this example, a part-time placement of four or three days a week will be spread over nine or twelve weeks, respectively. Some full-time placements require more time than is available in the degree programme (*e.g.* because of the nature of the activities). This will always extend the length of your studies, so at this step of the process you really need to consider whether you can afford this. Your study advisor can help you with this. Occasionally, placement extensions receive extra credits.

1.1.3 The Placement Period

In principle, students have to meet a number of course requirements before they can start their placement. Some degree programmes require you to have accumulated a minimum number of credits, while for others you need to have completed a particular course (or courses). The purpose of most placements is to put knowledge acquired in your programme into practice; if you do not yet possess the basic knowledge of your degree programme, you will often not be able to do your placement.

This is why a placement is normally completed at or near the end of a programme. Sometimes it is scheduled in a specific semester or trimester, but often it is not. If it is left to you, you might want to consider scheduling it as the very last course; after completing your thesis, dissertation, or other final-year paper. This has the following advantages:

- You will be able to enter the labour market directly after completing your placement; if your placement provider offers you a job, you can accept it without any problems (30% of students on placement find a job through their placement).
- You won't have to return to university to complete your thesis – a transition that many students find difficult both socially as well as in terms of self-discipline.

In some cases, longer placements may be divided so that one part falls under your degree programme and the other part falls under 'volunteer work'. This way, your degree programme will award you the total number of possible credits and you won't have to suffer any study delay. If you plan this carefully, you can be working for the placement-providing organization and graduate at the same time.

1.1.4   A Placement Abroad

When you undertake a placement in your own country you might still be forced to move. A placement with a government department, for example, requires you to find a room close to the country's political centre. You can sublet your own room for that particular period; there are various websites that can help you with that. However, do keep in mind that moving, even for a short period, comes with extra costs.

In many cases, you can also opt for a placement abroad. Even if you have already spent a period in a country other than your own, a placement abroad can still be an option. If you are following an entire degree programme abroad, it is generally possible to go on placement in a country other than your home country or country of study. In principle, an international placement is the same as a placement at home, but there's more you'll need to sort out, such as insurance, a visa, medical preparations, and, sometimes, taxes.

The *similarities* between a domestic and an international placement are as follows:

- Content-wise, an assignment abroad may be the same as an assignment in your own country.
- Both international and domestic placements offer the opportunity to explore the day-to-day business of an organization.

- In domestic as well as in international placements, you will be treated according to the level of your degree programme; you are expected to show independence.
- Your daily rhythm will be different from what you are used to, and you have to be punctual.
- You have to report about your work to the host institution as well as maintain contact with your faculty.
- You will have a professional relationship with colleagues based on the knowledge you acquired during your studies, you will be introduced to a corporate culture, and you will have to be able to carry out tasks under time pressure.
- Moreover, you will have to write your placement report and any additional products.

The main difference is that a placement abroad will let you experience all this in a different language and culture.

The *differences* between international placements and domestic placements add the following to the placement experience:
- You will learn to work independently in a different culture. You will be thrown in at the deep end, as it were, without family and friends to turn to, which means you will really get to know yourself and will also get used to new customs and languages more easily.
- You will create an international network that may be useful for your future career. If you already know what kind of job you want to pursue after you graduate, your network might help you find a job in that field.
- A placement abroad adds international experience to your CV or résumé, which is highly regarded by employers.

You should keep in mind, however, that preparations for a placement abroad involve a lot more than preparations for one at home. From the moment you decide to undertake a placement, it generally takes nine to twelve months to find one. Placements in Europe are usually easier to find than elsewhere, as regulations in European countries are more closely aligned than regulations outside Europe, where they differ from country to country. In the latter case, a visa is virtually always required. The application procedure for a visa may cover several months, which is sometimes even longer than the duration of the placement itself! More on this can be found on: <www.internshipguide.elevenpub.com>.

If you are planning to go to a country with a poor security situation, you should seek travel advice issued by your country's Ministry of Foreign Affairs or that of any other country with a reliable website (*e.g.* Australia). If a negative travel advice has been issued, your faculty will advise against going. However, if your degree programme trains you for situations like these (*e.g.* humanitarian assistance), your university might ask you not to participate in its insurance scheme and not to accept potential grants. Your faculty might still approve the placement, however, in which case you can still earn credits. See Step 4.

For information about placements at European institutions, go to the EU Trainee Programme (check <www.internshipguide.elevenpub.com>). Apply in time; procedures for the European Union take several months. A placement at an EU institution can be worth your while if you want to work there in the future; many people now working for the European Union started their careers that way.

1.1.5 Supervision

You will have two supervisors during your placement period: a lecturer on behalf of the degree programme and a supervisor on behalf of the host institution. The main focus of a placement is the learning aspect, so it is important that its supervision is in order. In most institutions of higher education, students are *project managers of their placement*. This means that it is your responsibility to arrange meetings with your supervisors during your time on placement, to negotiate how these meetings will be held, and to make sure that these meetings take place via webcam, e-mail, or phone.

Once you have found a placement, you have to arrange the time and frequency of the supervision meetings with both your supervisors. In most cases, the faculty will appoint a *supervising lecturer* for you. This lecturer will, sometimes in consultation with the Board of Examiners, approve your placement and sign the placement contract on behalf of the degree programme. Your supervisor's approval is often based on your placement plan. While many degree programmes have a standard form available for this purpose, others will want you to draw up your own. Please keep in mind that you can accept a placement position only after it has been approved by your supervising lecturer or the Board of Examiners.

The supervisor at the host institution – the organization or company where the placement takes place – will be referred to here as the *practical supervisor*. The practical supervisor is usually not chosen by the student but by the host institution. He or she will normally be the one who provides you with work assignments and will therefore act as your superior. The criteria that practical supervisors should meet will be discussed in Section 1.2.

Most degree programmes in the Netherlands stress the importance of a *placement contract*, which lays down the agreements made with the supervisors. Such a contract guarantees that you will be awarded the agreed number of credits once you earn a pass for your placement. Placement contracts are generally completed in duplicate and signed by all parties: the student, the placement provider (*i.e.* the practical supervisor), the supervising lecturer, and sometimes a school or faculty representative. The host institution and the university each keep an original copy; the student and supervising lecturer both receive a duplicate. The placement component of a final-year project generally also requires a contract. The host institutions often have contracts of their own, which can be signed in addition to the placement contracts provided by the degree programme. In many cases, the contract provided by the host institution only needs to be signed by the student, but the lecturer sometimes needs to sign it as well. See Step 6.

1.1.6   *Financial Matters*

Placements are expensive. You may have to rent a room in a different city, you may be faced with extra travel costs, or you may have to buy a suit for a conference. Sometimes, you have temporarily to resign from your part-time job, or postpone expensive course units to the next semester. Reimbursement of expenses made, be it whole or partial, is not a matter of course; not all organizations provide a monthly placement allowance, and sometimes you have to pay for travel costs and other expenses yourself. If the organization does provide a placement remuneration, the amount is usually only about €300 gross per month. Depending on your degree programme, though, you may receive a remuneration of up to €2,000 gross per month (*e.g.* Business Studies or Information Technology). Note, however, that the amount of your remuneration may change your status from 'student on placement' to 'employee'.

The extra costs of a placement abroad compared with a placement in your own country are rather obvious: travel expenses, rent, the higher costs of living expenses, visas, extra insurance, and, if necessary, vaccinations.

Whether or not all students can afford a placement is a fair question to ask. If you have plenty of time to search (in this case, time is money too), you can search as long as is necessary to find a placement-providing organization that offers a reasonable monthly remuneration. You can also try to negotiate a placement remuneration, or find out if it is possible to increase the proposed remuneration (by being compensated for travel or accommodation costs, for example). Some companies do not offer placement remunerations for fiscal reasons, but might instead give financial compensation for such things as laptops, books, and subscriptions.

If you receive a student grant in the Netherlands and your placement is a component of your degree programme, you will usually continue to receive this grant during your time on placement. For relevant conditions and regulations, you can consult the Dutch Education Executive Agency (DUO).

As mentioned above, you can sublet your room via websites specially designed for this purpose. These websites can also help you arrange a *room exchange* for a limited period. Some schools provide placement grants. Many universities offer an Erasmus grant for placements in Europe, for instance. Other possibilities are grant directories and websites, which offer grants for placements and other projects (go to <www.internshipguide.elevenpub.com> for more information).

In many cases, however, the only thing you can do is save up for a placement, perhaps by making some extra money with a part-time job.

1.2   The Content of the Placement

Once your questions about the preconditions have been answered, you can start looking for information about the content of the placement. After all, you want to know what kind of placement assignment you can do. Which tasks will you be allowed and not allowed to do?

The main purpose of a placement is to give you insight into the relationship between the degree programme and the professional work field. This means that the content of a placement should dovetail with the objectives of your degree programme. Questions that you might have are: in which professional field should my placement take place? Will I be allowed to do a teaching placement, for instance, or is policy advice the only option? Will I carry out tasks for the organization like a regular employee, as in an observational placement, or do I have to undertake a research project of my own?

You also have to find out what the outcome, the final product, of your placement should be. You probably have to hand in a placement report at the end of your placement, but do you also have to include a research assignment in your placement project? Are you always required to hand in an advisory report, or do you have to design a product, or draw up a market analysis, a treatment plan, or a communication plan?

1.2.1   *Learning Outcomes*

Before focusing on content-related requirements, students are often confronted with a number of learning outcomes. These are provided by your degree programme to acquaint you with the learning objectives.

For example: the placement provides you with the opportunity to gain practical experience in a social environment. The objectives of the placement are:

1. Testing the knowledge, attitude, and skills that you acquired in your degree programme against the practical environment of an organization.
2. Acquiring practical experience at the level of your degree programme, corresponding to the knowledge, insights, and skills acquired in the programme.
3. Learning more about a potential future profession or field.

Naturally, a student on placement should also make a contribution to the host institution. This could be anything and will be stated in the placement assignment.

Next, you will be presented with the competences to be acquired.

For example:
- The student takes in new situations, problems, and information, and processes these critically. The student utilizes new experiences effectively and is able to self-reflect. He can cope with criticism, asks for it where needed, and reacts adequately to it.
- The student continues to act efficiently by adapting to a changing environment, to changing responsibilities, or to other people.
- The student communicates ideas and information clearly and correctly, bearing in mind interlocutors, listeners, and readers, and in such a way that they receive and understand the message.
- The student is capable of directing his acts and decisions towards an active realization of qualitative and quantitative results in a professional organization, and aims at continuous improvements.

1.2.2   Placement Assignment Criteria

It is often difficult for students to recognize the required learning outcomes in a placement assignment. It is hard to determine whether a placement offered by a company (a) fits the level of your degree programme, and (b) is long enough to be awarded with credits. The best way to find out whether the placement meets your faculty's requirements would be to ask your lecturer.

Possible criteria for the placement assignment are, for example:
- The level of the placement activities is sufficient: the student should have the opportunity to carry out activities matching the level of his degree programme. Creativity and intelligence must be 'tested' at this level. Carrying out purely supporting secretarial or administrative activities is not allowed.
- The placement provides sufficient activities and input.

- The placement assignment is challenging, which means that:
    - the assignment draws on the student's analytical and problem-solving skills;
    - the assignment draws on the student's skills as regards searching, finding, and processing information;
    - the student is required to use his communication skills, both written and oral;
    - the student is required to work autonomously for most of the time.

Your lecturer or study advisor can advise you in these matters. In some cases, they can also help you table any non-standard placement plans to the Board of Examiners.

You are, in any case, advised to ask for sample placement assignments, which can sometimes be provided by senior students. Some degree programmes also allow students to access and consult previous placement reports. These may give you a clearer picture of potential projects and activities, as well as shed some light on the feasibility of the tasks that have to be carried out. After all, it is often difficult to estimate the amount of work that can be done in a period of, say, only three months.

Many degree programmes require students to look for a work placement themselves; this search is part of the learning process of professional orientation that characterizes a placement. If this applies to you, Step 1, 'Orientation', will be followed by Step 2, 'Self-Analysis'. Perhaps your faculty will look for a placement for or with you, or even lets you choose from a list of possible placements. If this applies to you, you can skip Step 3, 'Marketing Analysis', but it is still useful to follow Step 2, 'Self-Analysis'.

Conclusion

Orientation, the first step towards a placement, focuses on three questions: why do I want to go on placement, what are the degree programme's preconditions regarding work placements, and what are the requirements regarding the content of a placement? Hopefully, this step will give you a clear picture of your options as well as help you decide whether you want to go through with it. Below, you will find two sample placements to give you an idea of what to expect. One concerns a placement abroad, the other a placement in the Netherlands. These examples will paint a picture of the steps that may follow next. Sometimes it is possible, of course, to skip a step or parts of a step.

1.3   Examples

1.3.1   Example of an International Placement: Martin

Step 1: Orientation

The degree programme in International Business and Marketing in Groningen involves a compulsory placement abroad. Martin already knows at the start of his degree programme that he has to find one himself. In that sense, he has plenty of time to search. Also, since he considers a placement to be the most important programme component by far, he does not want to rush it. He decides to prepare his placement thoroughly, as he is convinced that a good placement will help determine his future. Nine months before the placement is scheduled to take place, Martin tries to decide which part of the world he would like to go to. It should definitely be an exotic location, and it should not be too close to home. As for many students following this international programme, his 'home' can refer to many different locations: the Netherlands, where he was born and where he lived till he was eight; the French side of the Antillean island of Saint Martin, where he lived from the age of eight until the age of seventeen; and Melbourne, in Florida, USA, where he went to high school.

Step 2: Self-Analysis

• Choice of Continent

During his studies, Martin meets his girlfriend Mieke, also a student of International Business and Marketing. She is going to look for a placement abroad too, but chances of their timing and choice of placement overlapping are slim. They decide to let their studies and choice of placement come first. After talking about it at length, Martin decides to fulfil his initial wish: to undertake a placement in an exotic location. He opts for Asia; he has never been there, and Asia has plenty of companies that could be of interest to his degree programme.

• Choice of Sector

The first step has been made: Martin has chosen a continent. The second step is actually easier than the first: choosing a sector. In his youth, which he spent in the Antilles, his great passion was windsurfing – and if the Dutch seawater had been a little warmer, he would still be windsurfing every day. Be that as it may, he is determined to undertake a placement with a surfing-equipment manufacturer. As an 'expert user', he knows exactly which companies provide quality material, so it does not take him long to come up with a shortlist: Tiga, Mistral, North, NeilPryde,

Gaastra, Fanatic, Cobra, and Aerotech. All he has to do now is find out which of these manufacturers have branches in Asia. Martin learns, from the Ministry of Economic Affairs, that the options are Hong Kong, Bangkok, Colombo (Sri Lanka), and Singapore.

• Choice of Country

By now, Martin has seven months until his placement begins. But the programme in International Business and Marketing requires students to first complete part of a comparable programme abroad during an exchange period before they are allowed to go on placement. This means that Martin has to study abroad for five months to earn credits for his degree programme at home. Because he wants to do his placement in Asia, he chooses an Asian destination from the list of exchange countries. His options are Thailand, Malaysia, and Macau. As he will be travelling to Asia anyway, he decides to continue his search for a placement there, during his exchange period. Over there, he will have become relatively used to the language and culture, and he will be able to conduct any interviews face-to-face. Note that this is his own reasoning. Until now, he has not yet discussed the content of his choice of placement with his department. He is an early bird, so to speak, because he really wants his placement to be exactly as he has in mind. As Martin has already figured out which surfing companies have branches in Asia, he crosses Thailand and Malaysia from the list; the chance that he would find a placement with a leading surfing manufacturer in one of those two countries is simply too small. The country that remains is Macau, near Hong Kong, with branches of three out of the four major windsurfing manufacturers (NeilPryde, Gaastra, and Fanatic).

• Open Ending
Martin won't be seeing his girlfriend for at least five months. She and their fellow students are going to spend their exchange period in different places. Only two other classmates will be staying in Macau at the same time as Martin. When Martin takes leave of Mieke, he knows that he will probably be gone for more than five months. He has already agreed with his study advisor to extend his stay by another three months if he succeeds in finding a placement in or around Macau. His open-year ticket makes this possible.

Step 3: Market Analysis

Once in Macau, Martin draws up a list of thirty international organizations that would qualify as placement provider. Apart from the surfing manufacturers that he had already looked up in the Netherlands, the list includes banks, trading companies, and textile factories. He then ranks the thirty companies from most to least interesting placement provider using a number of criteria: first, of course, is it a surfing company? Second, what is its location? He has already seen some of the companies on his travels through the densely populated city-state Hong Kong, near Macau. Thus he knows what they look like and whether they are easy to get to from the neighbourhood where he's staying. The other companies are situated in the suburbs. He has not seen them, and they would require a lot of travel time every day. Martin's third criterion is the working language: if it is a truly international company, with its headquarters in the United States or Europe, the working language will be English, just as in Hong Kong. At companies that are Asian in origin, many employees will be able to speak English, but chances are that the actual working language is Cantonese or Mandarin Chinese. Martin's last criterion is size. Branches with fewer than forty employees end up at the bottom of his list, as do companies with more than 500. Using these four selection criteria, Martin ends up with a ranked list of thirty companies.

27

Step 4: Networking

Now that he has a list on his laptop ranking the potential placement providers, Martin is ready to start applying. He wants to do this thoroughly; he does not want to make any mistakes when applying to the highest-ranking companies, so he decides to use the fifteen lowest-ranking companies as 'practice material'. He starts networking. By applying to these companies he may discover the most successful way of finding a placement in Hong Kong. He calls the personnel departments of three companies to inquire about their business activities. He explains that he studies International Business and Marketing and is looking for a work placement. It strikes him that he has to spend a lot of time explaining that he is not looking for a paid job. None of the three personnel managers have ever heard of the terms 'placement' or 'internship'. One of them keeps repeating that there are no vacancies, the other says that their company is in a hiring freeze, and the third does not understand that Martin *really* does not mind not getting paid. The concept of an unpaid placement as part of a degree programme is unknown in Hong Kong. With this information, Martin continues. He needs a different approach. Just sending an open application will not work in this city. The best way to make an appointment would be to send a custom letter followed by a follow-up call. Martin discovers that he can capture the addressee's attention with a letter without giving away too much about what he really wants . . . This way, he does not put off the reader, but does succeed in making an appointment.

Step 5: Applying for a Placement

In the second 'application round' during the five months he spends on exchange in Macau, Martin takes a different, more personal approach. He decides to contact the companies by phone instead of writing a letter first. He calls them and tries to get to speak to their personnel manager. If after four attempts he still does not get to speak to the staff officer concerned personally, Martin crosses the company off his list. After several phone calls, he learns that they respond in a much friendlier manner if he takes the time to explain that he, as a Dutch 'applied science' student of International Business and Marketing, is looking for a 'training period' in Hong Kong. This approach is successful even when he explains that he does not need to get paid. Three of the managers he speaks to would like to see a motivation letter and CV. However, they all stress that they are not sure whether they will be able to provide a placement for him, and they first wish to consult their company's relevant departments: the Sales department and the Marketing department, respectively.

After sending off the letters, Martin waits three weeks. None of the personnel managers have replied. He decides to call again. He manages to get the three staff officers on the phone again, and it turns out that two of them have not yet spoken to their Marketing department. They are having a meeting first. The third personnel manager decides not to explain further the concept of 'placement' within his company. This gives Martin another illuminating idea: perhaps it would be better to contact the Marketing departments himself, instead of waiting for the personnel departments to do this for him. This could also considerably reduce the 'noise' in the communication process; the personnel departments might misinterpret the unknown concept of 'placement' . . .

Step 6: The Interview

After having practised on twenty-five companies (at three of them he was even selected successfully), Martin decides it is time to approach his top five favourite companies. After making the necessary phone calls and writing the necessary letters, Martin pays a visit to each company; naturally, he wants to see where he might be ending up. He finally arrives at his favourite company, NeilPryde, where he gets to meet the personnel manager who – as usual – doesn't really understand Martin's request. Martin now knows how to deal with this, however, and manages to convince her. The woman realizes that she would be making a good deal by taking Martin on because he would be working for a remuneration instead of a salary. She therefore decides to call the marketing manager, who thinks the whole undertaking is a fun idea and asks Martin when he could start. After only three weeks, Martin starts with his dream placement.

Step 7: The Placement

Martin's university of applied sciences provides him with a standard placement agreement, which NeilPryde only needs to copy and sign. The agreement provides insurance details and other information, including the address of the placement office, so most of the formal arrangements have been accounted for. Martin is responsible for his visa. In exchange for the placement, the host institution pays the rent of Martin's flat for the duration of the placement. In addition, Martin is required to comply with the rules and working hours of the company, of course, just like the other employees.

The placement itself runs smoothly. Martin proposes to carry out an evaluation for the company, in addition to the assignment they already agreed upon. All compulsory components of his degree programme are covered in this evaluation. Martin also carries out various unplanned tasks at the request of his supervisor. It is up to him to decide whether he has time to do these tasks in addition to the assignment and the evaluation.

Step 8: Rounding Off Your Placement

The new marketing manager is very busy. After only two weeks, he hands Martin an extra assignment larger than the others: to prepare the annual internal catalogue of all their products. Martin decides to accept the assignment even though this would mean he has to work longer days. As a result, they ask him after only three weeks if he would like to stay on after the initial placement period; the department could use a go-getter like him. After consulting with his supervising teacher, Martin succeeds in extending his placement. He gets permission to do his last semester from Hong Kong, but he does have to return home every few months for his exams.

1.3.2   Example of a Dutch Placement: Susan

Step 1: Orientation

Susan's degree programme in Communication involves a compulsory five-month placement. It is going to be her final-year project, the final stage of her programme, but a year before it is scheduled to begin she has no idea yet what she would like to do. Her placement assignment consists of writing an advisory report for an organization in one of the fields of communication. She is allowed to choose her own host institution. In order to prepare for her search, she has the following three documents at her disposal: a manual on how to compile a final project advisory report, a set of instructions telling her how to formulate a Plan of Action for a work placement, and a list of just fifteen examples of final-year placements.

The first document, the manual, will not be very useful in the orientation phase; it will not help her define what she wants to do, only what she *needs* to do. The second document, which has been posted on Blackboard (her faculty's digital learning environment), asks for a situation analysis and a choice of competences she wants to acquire; she can choose from thirty competences listed in the course catalogue. She dismisses the third document, the list of sample placements, because she thinks it is too limited.

Susan thinks back to her third year, when she did a five-month observational placement with the marketing department of a national newspaper. Back then, it was the faculty that found her the placement, which made things a lot easier; now, she has no idea where to start. She feels that the degree programme is leaving her to her own devices, while more and more fellow students around her seem to be able to find final-year placements.

She decides to go over the preconditions once again. The placement must take place between February and July. If she doesn't succeed in having a placement approved by that time, it will have to be postponed to September. The host organization must be willing to let her write an advisory report, which should be based on research and include practical tips for the host organization. Next on the list is the location of the placement. Her third-year placement was in Amsterdam, which required her to move from Tilburg. That was a costly affair, so she would like to stay closer to home this time. She will therefore look around in her area. Using these starting points, she returns to the documents provided by the degree programme.

Step 2: Self-Analysis

Susan tries to get started with the Plan of Action by first having a look at the competences listed in the course catalogue, reasoning that this might help her make a choice. She chooses five competences from the list and writes these down, but does not really know how this is going to help her find a placement provider.

Step 3: Market Analysis

Susan tells her friends on chat about her dilemma; how did they find a suitable company? She also poses this question to her placement coordinator. Time is running short, but she still has no idea which organization to approach. She fears that the credit crunch, very topical at that moment, is throwing a spanner in the works, and she does not know which sectors still accept students on placement. The placement coordinator refers her to the list of fifteen sample placements again; maybe there is something in there for her?

Running out of ideas, Susan goes through the online list of final-year placements again. Her eyes fall on a placement at a museum. While reading the description, she notices that she is gradually regaining her enthusiasm. She realizes that she has been placing too many limits on herself: all the while she had been under the impression that the placement had to be at a commercial organization, an idea that did not really appeal to her. She never realized until now that museums have communication departments too, and that they too have work placement opportunities. Yes, a placement at a museum sounds like a good idea.

Step 4: Networking

It is early December now, and Susan decides to take action right away. Before she can continue with her Plan of Action, she would first need to find a potential work placement anyway. She forgets to take the time to ask someone within or close to her network for help, and dives straight into the application process.

Step 5: Applying for a Placement

Susan sets to work vigorously now. She calls up all the museums in her area to ask them about the possibilities regarding a communications-related placement. The two largest museums do not have any places left. A staff member of a small museum Susan had never even heard of advises her to send an e-mail to the museum's education officer; Susan's question is instantly greeted with an enthusiastic response. There are several research plans that need to be carried out, and Susan is invited to discuss their suitability for her final-year project.

31

Step 6: The Interview

It turns out that the meeting between Susan and the education officer is not really an interview; the museum is glad to have her and Susan is free to choose what she wants to do. The museum welcomes her knowledge and dedication, and Susan agrees with the education officer to work on an external research project on potential target groups. She is going to investigate why certain groups of people (like herself) have never heard of the museum before, and what the museum can do to motivate these people to pay the museum a visit – in other words, a marketing issue.

Step 7: The Placement

Susan is enthusiastic about the project and wants to start immediately, but she has to ask her placement coordinator for approval first. He gives verbal approval and refers her to a lecturer. A form is needed to formalize the approval, but the academic counsellor first needs to check whether Susan has earned sufficient credits; there is a form available for this, too. Susan has to write down her problem definition on the approval form, including the host institution's contact information. She arranges an introductory meeting with the lecturer to discuss the problem definition. Meanwhile, she has to wait for over two weeks before she can tell the museum that the placement is really going to take place.

During the introductory meeting, Susan discusses not only the problem definition with the lecturer, but also planning. The first two weeks will be spent working at the museum's Education department to let all the aspects of the work sink in and to find out what role she could be playing there. Once the first two weeks are over, Susan has to round off her Plan of Action. She discusses the Plan with the education officer, after which she e-mails it to her lecturer. The lecturer then pays a visit to the placement site. During a meeting between the lecturer (external placement supervisor), the education officer (internal placement supervisor), and Susan, the plan is finalized. Susan completes the placement contract so that they can sign it immediately.

While drawing up her Plan of Action, Susan still has doubts about her placement; not about her choice of placement provider this time, but about her approach. Initially, she feels insecure about her approach and plans, and she has the feeling that a lot is expected of her. Fortunately, she can discuss these doubts with her internal placement supervisor. She feels that she cannot really talk to her lecturer about these doubts because he is the one who is eventually going to assess her placement.

For Susan, the highlight of the placement takes place halfway through it. The faculty has organized a follow-up day in Tilburg in early April for all students on placement to get together and share their experiences without their supervisors being present.

Prior to the follow-up day, all students have been asked to prepare an assignment. They have to answer five questions on a sheet of paper:

- Who is your placement provider?
- What is your assignment?
- What do you think of the supervision provided by your university and the organization?
- What issues do you encounter?
- How far along are you?

The answers are discussed in groups of eight. To Susan's relief, everyone in her group is just as far along as she is, and they all have occasional doubts about their role and contribution. She really likes and appreciates the timing and set-up of the follow-up day. The day yielded a wealth of information and was also a lot of fun!

Step 8: Rounding Off Your Placement

The manual on writing a final project advisory report comes in handy when Susan is rounding off her placement. No less than nine pages explain in detail which sections should be included in the advisory report and how to make a distinction between the research component and the advisory component of your report. After discussing the draft report with her internal supervisor, she e-mails it to her teacher. He replies by e-mail. Susan revises the report and prints it.

The final interview requires yet another form, and it has to take place no later than two weeks before the date on which Susan wishes to graduate. This causes her some stress, just as in the beginning. The lecturer checks the report against the list of competences and, once an external expert from the field has been found, it is time for the final interview. Susan does not really know how to prepare, which also has to do with the fact that the external expert is a stranger. She worries about how to present herself during the interview, but it turns out to be a pleasant meeting and she receives final approval. She can now apply for her degree certificate!

Step 2 Self-Analysis

Once you are familiar with the formal, content-related criteria, you are faced with the question of what you want your placement to include. Your study advisor might ask you any of the following questions: What would you like to do? What type of job are you interested in? What type of organization are you interested in? Would you like to undertake a placement with a commercial company, or would you prefer a non-profit organization? Would you be interested in a government organization, or does your heart go out to a small non-governmental organization (NGO)? Would you rather work for a small organization or for a large company? If you do not have an answer to any of these questions yet, other possible questions could be: What would you like your placement to prepare you for? What would you like to do after you graduate? Where would you like to work in the future?

These are all relevant questions, but your head will probably be filling up with question marks rather than answers. There are probably a lot of questions that you would like to have answered first, such as: what type of organization would take on someone like me? What qualities do I have that would allow me to succeed there? What qualities make me suitable for a placement within a commercial organization or government organization? How will I know whether I'm more suitable for a small or a large organization?

It's all these questions that make the second step the biggest step of the placement-searching process. If you have not yet spent any time on figuring out who you really are, what your abilities are, and what you want your role in the labour market to be, then a lot remains to be done. But at least the work involved in this step is pleasant: it allows you to be completely self-involved for a while without yet having to concern yourself too much with the placement. You should first focus inwards for a moment and become aware of the limitations you have imposed on yourself. Next, you will have to take a close look at your personality. You will then be able to find out what kinds of tasks you prefer to do, and with this knowledge you can figure out which sectors, industries, companies, and professions fit your characteristics and wishes.

2.1 Who Am I?

'Become who you are' is the motto that Nobiles, an organization for job seekers, once used in their campaign to promote a career event. Isn't that what everybody wants?

Whether you are who you are or not, it's almost impossible to complete the first step towards a placement without having a good look at yourself first (instead of looking out).

2.1.1 Boundaries and Barriers

You can avoid a lot of trouble by taking the time to look at yourself. There's nothing worse than working on a placement from 9 to 5 (or longer) every day if you don't feel comfortable with the organization. It can make you really unhappy, which, in turn, has a negative influence on your performance.

The problem with this substep is that everyone tends to impose restrictions on themselves, especially when they lack the necessary information or knowledge of a situation, which can lead to too much thinking 'inside the box'. People tend to impose barriers on themselves as a means of self-preservation, while it often turns out that these barriers need not exist at all.

Anna enters the placement office. 'After thinking long and hard,' she says, 'I have decided that I want to do a placement after all. What now?' The placement coordinator asks her what she studies. 'German Studies,' Anna replies. 'So you want to go on placement in Germany?' the placement coordinator suggests tentatively. 'No,' says Anna, shocked. 'Absolutely not.' She says that the decision to go on placement is a major decision for her as it is. She still lives with her parents in Copenhagen and also goes to university there, so to live on her own elsewhere in Denmark for a while would be a big enough step in itself. She fears that taking that extra step over the border would be too radical a change for her. She has clearly done a lot of thinking about what she does *not* want to do. The placement coordinator tells her that she could also undertake a placement just across the border; that way, she will be able to brush up on her German . . . But Anna is very determined. After discussing a number of placement possibilities in Denmark, she goes home to think about it some more. Two weeks later she's back. 'I have been thinking it over again, and I want to go to Germany after all!' It turns out she found a placement with an agency that focuses on cooperation between Denmark and Germany, 320 km from her university. She can speak Danish there but will be living among Germans, and the assignment dovetails with her degree programme. The placement coordinator compliments her on finding this wonderful opportunity. She beams. 'It's quite daunting, but I think I have made the right choice.' When Anna steps into the office four months later, the placement coordinator does not recognize her at first; standing in front of him is a confident, grown-up woman. 'It's me, Anna!' The four months in Germany have clearly done her good, and she proudly publishes her placement report on the website of her degree programme – *with* a big photo.

But it may also be the other way round: students may think that a certain type of company would be fun to work at, yet have no idea where their degree programme and experience would come in. They too are guided by perceptions that are not based on facts.

John goes to his lecturer to discuss the upcoming academic year. He wants to take up a placement as an optional module for his degree programme in American Studies because he's heard that gaining experience that dovetails with your programme looks good on your résumé. 'What kind of placement do you have in mind?' the lecturer asks. John is thinking about a placement at a publishing house or a school. The lecturer is surprised: 'Are you aware that these two are very different from each other? As, for that reason, are the roles of language students there?' John admits that he did not know that. He simply does not know anyone who is a publisher or teacher.

And then there are students who have the omnipotent feeling that the world lies at their feet: they have wide-ranging interests and consider this a great advantage.

> Joline walks in cheerfully with a tanned face, hair hanging loose, long earrings, and a flamboyant coat. She has put a lot of thought into this and also discussed it at length with her friends: she wants to do a placement abroad. When the placement coordinator asks her where she would like to go, she says that she does not really care. She thinks it would be good to live abroad for a while and experience a different culture. But what is she aiming for? Well, that's the problem . . . She has already been looking through some vacancies, but there is nothing that she *doesn't* like. She wants to do something with development co-ordination but would also like to work at an embassy. And she has a friend who is doing a placement with Heineken, which sounds like fun too . . .

2.1.2 *People Around You*

The best way to get to know yourself is to talk to family, colleagues, and friends. The way they know you, at work or in private, is who you are. Below you will find an instructive, and therefore sometimes confronting, exercise:

> **Exercise: Asking People Around You How They See You**
> Pick three people and ask them the following questions. Try to pick someone from work (*e.g.* a colleague at your part-time job) as well as someone from your private life. Only ask people whose answers you are really interested in.

1. What, in your opinion, are my strongest qualities?
   a. When do I demonstrate these qualities?
   b. Why do you value these qualities?
2. Which of the qualities that I already possess should I, in your opinion, develop further?
3. Can you name three aspects of my behaviour that you think I should change?

2.1.3   Models and Tests

Perhaps you do not yet sufficiently recognize yourself in the answers provided by these people. It is often like listening to a recording of your own voice: your voice on a recording (your outside voice) is different from the voice you hear when you are talking (your inside voice). You probably also want to find out *for yourself* what the characteristics of your personality type are.

A good way to get to know yourself better is to do a test. Questionnaires are easily available, for instance on the Internet or at career centres, and can be filled in at your own leisure. It is important that you receive feedback on these tests, given by a professional career coach who discusses the test results with you in person. Such coaches are qualified to interpret the results and can tell you in which direction you could start looking for a job or a placement. It's not a good idea to do these tests without feedback. Online personality tests, for instance, yield digital results that are probably not very helpful. They can make you feel insecure and often raise new questions instead of giving you a clearer idea of what your qualities are.

The Big Five
An example of a personality test is the 'mini Big Five', which is derived from the well-known, patented (and therefore not free) Big Five test.

The Mini Big Five

		Very in-accurate	Some-what inaccu-rate	Neither accurate nor inac-curate	Accurate	Very accurate
1	When I'm at a party, I talk to many different people.	--	-	-/+	+	++
2	I worry about things.	--	-	-/+	+	++
3	My room is untidy.	--	-	-/+	+	++
4	I have a vivid imagination.	--	-	-/+	+	++

5	I don't like being the centre of attention.	--	-	-/+	+	++
6	I make time for other people.	--	-	-/+	+	++
7	I work to a time schedule.	--	-	-/+	+	++
8	I am rarely irritated.	--	-	-/+	+	++
9	I think of others first.	--	-	-/+	+	++
10	I find it hard to imagine things.	--	-	-/+	+	++
11	I let others take the lead.	--	-	-/+	+	++
12	I am always prepared.	--	-	-/+	+	++
13	I take discussions to a higher level.	--	-	-/+	+	++
14	I am usually relaxed.	--	-	-/+	+	++
15	I make people feel at ease.	--	-	-/+	+	++
16	I complain about things.	--	-	-/+	+	++
17	I sense other people's emotions.	--	-	-/+	+	++
18	I shirk my duties.	--	-	-/+	+	++
19	I don't mind being the centre of attention.	--	-	-/+	+	++
20	I can process a lot of information at once.	--	-	-/+	+	++

Source: <www.intermediair.nl>

The answers result in scores on five scales: emotional stability, agreeableness, conscientiousness, the need for social stimuli, and originality and intellect. Personality psychologists are interested in how one person differs from another and why we behave the way we do. Personality research, like any science, relies on quantifiable, concrete data that can be used to examine what people are like. This is where the Big Five test plays an important role.

There are many more tests like these, however. It's possible that your careers advisor uses a different test. This is okay, as long as he or she is a registered and experienced career consultant. What counts, after all, is the combination of your personal presentation and vision and the test results. For a list of tests and career coaches, go to <www.internshipguide.elevenpub.com>.

2.1.4 Your Basic CV

There's an easy way to discover what your characteristics are without having to spend money on a careers advice centre to have a test assessed for you. It takes some time, but it will give you some tools that allow you to enter the labour market with confidence.

You begin the introspection phase by creating a basic curriculum vitae (CV).[2] This is a summary of your experience and skills. Without yet having to worry about the format requirements discussed in Step 3, you can start with a little brainstorming. Sit down with a blank page or at a blank computer screen and try to remember the experiences, training, courses, and activities you've had or done since leaving secondary school. From your part-time job as a dishwasher to organizing an information evening, from a photography course to travelling through Latin America: write down *everything*. Leave nothing out and take all your activities seriously because everything you've undertaken can help you figure out who you are. Put the results of your brainstorming session aside for a day because you'll definitely come up with more in the following days. Do write them down as soon as they pop up or you might forget them.

The result is an outline of your basic CV. First, arrange the activities in chronological order. Put the earliest activity at the top and the most recent activity at the bottom. Put your personal details at the top of the page followed by the degree programmes you have completed, including the year of graduation. The activities can be divided and grouped under the headings 'other courses and training' and 'work experience'.

2.2   What Are My Competences?

Now that you have an overview of your activities, you can start defining your *characteristics* by looking at your behaviour in the various activities in which you were involved. However, it's not always easy to determine which characteristics are associated with a particular type of behaviour. How would you know if you are stress resilient, for instance? Or open? Or proactive?

Everyone possesses characteristics like those, even if people do not use those terms when describing you. Are you the friend who always remains calm when others are having trouble? Who lightens the mood but also calls for help and makes sure that you and your friends can continue as usual? This means you are stress resilient. When you are faced with a problem, do you talk about it with others in order to find a solution? This means you have an open personality. Are you the first one in your project group to contact the lecturer if there are questions about the assignment? This means you are proactive.

---

2   In the United States and Australia, a CV is called a résumé. In this guide we refer to this tool as a 'CV'.

From all these experiences you can distil a number of characteristics that apply to you. These are your *competences*. This term is more accurate in this context than *characteristics* because it refers to something that can be acquired. It is also the term used by employers. There are many definitions of the word *competence*, but we will use this one:

> A competence is a quality that can be used in a variety of authentic contexts, based on the integrated application of knowledge, rules and guidelines, techniques, procedures, skills, insight, attitude, and values. Every competence thus represents a dynamic combination of knowledge, insight, skills, and attitude, and can be acquired in many different contexts. (freely rendered from Villa Sánchez and Poblete Ruiz, 2008: 29)

The table below provides a number of examples:

Activity	Competences
Committee work	Commitment, team spirit, an interest in policy, communication skills
Leading a youth camp	Ability to work under stress, organizational talent, creativity
Studying abroad	Independence, initiative, pioneering spirit
Combining a top-level sport with your studies	Perseverance
A summer job	Commitment, motivation, independence
Raising sponsorship money	Commercial understanding

Competences Assigned to the Performed Activities

2.2.1   Generic Competences

There are roughly two types of competences: subject-specific competences and generic competences. Subject-specific competences are directly related to your field of study. You can find them in your course catalogue under the descriptions of the course units' learning outcomes. Generic competences fall outside the confines of a degree programme and are therefore also known as *transversal/transferable skills*: they are not directly subject-related. However, they can be interpreted as subject-specific in the context of a degree programme or work environment. For instance, the generic competence 'working in a team' can be considered a subject-specific competence in the context of a degree programme in Business and Management.

This book addresses only generic competences because they can be a great help in determining whether your personality matches a potential placement or host institution. You can also use them in a placement interview (Step 6), for example when answering questions about your personality or when discussing a case. In that respect, generic competences are useful for every step in the placement process. They are called *generic* because they are competences that you have acquired during *a wide range of activities in your life*: jobs, classes, projects, hobbies, sports, etc. – virtually anything that is transferable and applicable to what you want to do in your placement or future job.

Five types of generic competences will be mentioned here: communicative competences, competences in the field of research and planning, competences in the area of human relations, competences in the field of organization, management, and leadership, and work-related competences (see also <www.internshipguide. elevenpub.com>).

Generic communicative competences: the skilful expression, transmission and interpretation of knowledge and ideas. For example:
- speaking and presenting effectively
- writing concisely
- listening attentively
- expressing your thoughts
- facilitating group discussion
- providing appropriate feedback
- negotiating
- perceiving non-verbal messages
- persuading
- reporting information
- describing feelings
- interviewing
- editing

Example
My work as a telemarketer required me to communicate with a diverse array of people, some of whom presented me with difficult challenges. I had to refine my communication skills to the point where I was nearly always able to smooth ruffled feathers, solve problems, and provide satisfaction to customers. These are exactly the skills that are vital to effective hotel management, and I am eager to apply my talents at your hotel.

Generic competences in the field of research and planning: the search for specific knowledge and the ability to conceptualize future needs and solutions for meeting those needs. For example:

- predicting, anticipating
- creating ideas
- identifying problems
- imagining alternatives
- thinking outside the box
- identifying resources
- gathering information
- solving problems
- setting goals
- extracting important information
- defining needs
- analyzing
- developing evaluation strategies

> **Example**
> The office clerk job I held for three summers in my former hometown demanded a high degree of organization and detail-orientation. My former employer can affirm that I am fully capable of applying these important skills at your accounting firm. My experience also taught me the importance of fitting into the office culture, and I stand ready to become a contributing member of your team.

Generic competences in the area of human relations: the use of interpersonal skills for resolving conflict, relating to people, and helping people.

- developing reports
- being sensitive
- listening
- conveying feelings
- asserting
- providing support for others
- motivating
- counselling
- cooperating
- delegating with respect
- representing others
- perceiving feelings, situations

> **Example**
> As a sales associate in a retail store, I successfully handled customers' needs every day. To succeed, I had to be a patient and diplomatic problem-solver. Because the same kinds of patience and creative problem-solving are required of teachers, I am confident I will be an effective third-grade teacher at your school.

43

Generic competences in the field of organization, management, and leadership: the ability to supervise, direct, and guide individuals and groups in the completion of tasks and fulfilment of goals.

- initiating new ideas
- coordinating tasks
- managing groups
- delegating responsibility
- managing conflict
- teaching
- coaching
- counselling
- promoting change
- selling ideas or products
- decision-making with others
- being patient

> ### Example
> My work-study position as a computer-lab assistant involved a solid knowledge of the technology within the labs as well as the ability to teach that technology to fellow students, and the skills to assist those who had problems with the software and hardware. I would like to do a placement with your consultancy mainly because I expect to be able to use my competences there. I possess the knowledge to assist clients, as well as the interpersonal skills to do so successfully.

Generic work-related competences: the day-to-day skills that assist in promoting effective production and work satisfaction.

- implementing decisions
- cooperating
- enforcing policies
- being punctual
- managing time
- attending to detail
- meeting goals
- enlisting help
- accepting responsibility
- setting and meeting deadlines
- organizing
- making decisions

> ### Example
> As a former carer to three active youngsters, I certainly know the importance of good *time management*. I've gained that skill, along with exemplary leader

ship, organizational, and communication talents. I think that these competences would contribute to our mutual success if I join your management trainee programme.

2.2.2 Your Personal Profile

The combination of what your friends and family say about you, the results of a possible personality test, and your basic CV form your personal profile: an overview of your qualities in terms of competences. This is useful because many organizations think in terms of competences.

You can compile your competences into a list. Here is an example:

Example of a List of Competences of a Communications Expert
- Works methodically
- Good written and oral skills
- Proactive
- Analytical ability
- Adaptability
- Result-driven

This is not all, however. Many of your fellow students have been following practically the same study programme as you (at least, in the eyes of an outsider, *i.e.* an employer) and will have a list of competences similar to yours. Compiling your personal profile is about discovering what distinguishes you from others. Another example:

Example of a Summarized Personal Profile of a Communications Expert

As a communications expert, I am good at analysing communication processes within organizations. I take pleasure in formulating projects that can contribute to the optimization of communication within an organization. I am proficient in drawing up and monitoring plans, but always keep an eye on the people whom it concerns. My flexibility allows me to make adjustments according to their needs. I like exchanging ideas with them about the process, both in writing and orally. However, I make sure never to lose sight of the aim of the project; when I start something, I like to finish it successfully.

Your personal profile tells a great deal about you, but not everything. For instance, it says nothing about the *values* you look for in a placement or job. Few people take this into consideration when looking for work, strangely enough. Most people go no further than exploring their skills, knowledge, and interests (as described above). If you start searching for a placement purely based on those criteria you can still wind up disappointed. After all, even if a placement exactly matches your knowledge and interests, you might still feel unhappy if your way of working fits in badly with the organization. In addition to knowing what you are capable of, you also need to know what you want.

2.3   What Do I Want? (And What Don't I Want?)

All organizations unconsciously represent an entire system of norms and values endorsed by management. If these norms and values are largely incompatible with yours, then this is bound to become a problem. A way to determine whether an organization suits you is to find out if it shares your norms and values. To do this, you should first identify your *career values*.

Career values are personal values and characteristics (including job characteristics) that you deem important and would like to pursue in your work. For example: 'I want to be able to share my knowledge and experience', or 'I want to be financially independent.' <www.internshipguide.elevenpub.com> provides an extensive list of career values. Place together the ten career values to which you added '++' most spontaneously, and you will get an overview of the career values that you deem most important for your placement (and work). You can consider them as themes to reflect upon. If these values are not or insufficiently present in your work, you will start feeling uncomfortable with your job after a while; in that case, you should try and change the situation in consultation with your supervisor.

The list of career values helps you determine what you *want*. To illustrate, here's Maryse; curiously enough, she doesn't know that she already knows what she wants.

Maryse, a student of Communication Studies, wants to include a placement as an optional module in her Master's degree programme. She has wide-ranging interests and is willing to take on anything. For her, it is about gaining practical experience, but most of all about putting into practice the knowledge she acquired throughout the programme. The study advisor asks her what she is interested in: internal or external communication, marketing, or teaching? Maryse heaves a sigh and says: 'That's the problem: I don't know!' She is taking courses in all these fields, but seems unable to make up her mind. Isn't there anything that makes her heart beat faster? No, she really likes *everything*. When asked if she had to choose a subject for her research module, she beams. 'Yes!' she says, her eyes sparkling. 'I conducted a literature survey on an Indian tribe in Paraguay. No new studies have been conducted on this tribe since 1972. I would really like to do something with that; the tribe uses very interesting communication

methods ...' 'Well, what stops you?' the study advisor asks. 'Perhaps there is a
university or institute in Paraguay that would like to offer you a placement. We
can even arrange a travel grant for you.' Maryse leaves the study advisor's office
in relief; she is going to fulfil her dreams.

Finally, this is a good moment to consider whether you see your placement as the
first step towards a clearly defined career, or as an opportunity to spend some time
working in a fun place where you can put your talents to work. Perhaps your personality and choice of study would make you an excellent editorial assistant in a
current affairs programme on television, but you *really* don't want to work after
5 p.m. Do you want to have time to explore the area, to study, or to learn the language? Then you shouldn't look for a placement where you are expected to work
weeks that are closer to 50 hours than to 36. Do you want your placement to be
the first step towards a job in that organization? Then you should not undertake
a placement with a company that has a flat organizational structure, but rather
look for a large company where various departments can provide opportunities for
career advancement. The next step will outline this in more detail.

Conclusion

The self-analysis step provides you with the tools to draw up a personal profile that
identifies your competences. In order to learn to identify your competences, you
need to have an idea of your boundaries and barriers, to have an overview of all
your activities (your CV or résumé), and to have analyzed your strengths and weaknesses. Employers also speak in terms of competences in their job descriptions; to
speak in terms of competences is to speak the language of an organization. You can
add your list of competences to your personal profile, thus displaying your abilities
and wishes; a prerequisite when you start exploring the labour market in search of
a placement (Step 3).

47

Step 3 Market Analysis

You may not realize it, but if you are ready for the third step, market analysis, you have already made a lot of progress. By now, you probably know *what you want* and *what you are capable of,* and determining the latter is quite difficult as it is.

When you start looking for a placement, you obviously do not yet know exactly how it is going to help you find a job after you graduate. Perhaps thinking about how you are going to earn a living in the future is not important to you. Perhaps you just want your future job to be fun, or nearby, or easy to find.

However, you should realize that the future is not all that far away once you've started your search for a placement. You have to consider the experience gained during your placement period as (your first) work experience. This component of your CV in particular will be highly regarded by future employers and clients. They will want to know why you chose to work for that particular organization and why you chose that type of work because it tells them something about you. For that reason, doing something that you are passionate about and that fits your talents is not only important for you to be able to enjoy your placement; by formulating your talents and passions in your CV, you show placement providers and employers what inspires you and what you are good at.

This requires self-analysis. You might already have done some of that in Step 2 in drawing up a personal development profile. That profile helps you answer the question 'what kind of placement do I want to do?' It is important that the assignment, the organization, and the industry match your profile. The second stage of the preparation process is to search for sectors, industries, and companies that correspond to your profile: a market analysis.

3.1 The Organization

Strangely enough, students looking for a placement are hardly ever interested in the company offering a placement position. They are more interested in the assignment and the extent to which it fits their degree programme. The sector or industry in which a company operates is not always taken into consideration either. Still, it is a good idea to take a *helicopter view* before starting your search. Being aware of the role of your potential host institution within a group or several groups of organizations tells you more about the role that you can play there yourself.

3.1.1 Sector and Industry

Apart from choosing between a placement with a profit-making company and one with a government organization, you should also consider – when choosing the former – whether you would rather work in manufacturing or in the agriculture or forestry, or fishing sector. Additionally, you should be aware that the manufacturing sector and the agriculture, forestry, and fishing sector are very different from the business services sector, and therefore attract different types of people.

The Dutch Chamber of Commerce lists the various sectors as follows:

Standard Industrial Classifications (Dutch SBI 2008)
A   Agriculture, forestry, and fishing
B   Mining and quarrying
C   Manufacturing
D   Electricity, gas, steam, and air conditioning supply
E   Water supply; sewerage, waste management, and remediation activities
F   Construction
G   Wholesale and retail trade; repair of motor vehicles and motorcycles
H   Transportation and storage
I   Accommodation and food service activities
J   Information and communication
K   Financial institutions

L   Renting, buying, and selling of real estate
M   Consultancy, research, and other specialized business services
N   Renting and leasing of tangible goods and other business support services
O   Public administration, public services, and compulsory social security
P   Education
Q   Human health and social work activities
R   Culture, sports, and recreation
S   Other service activities
T   Activities of households as employers; undifferentiated goods- and service-producing activities of households for own use
U   Extraterritorial organizations and bodies
(*Source: Statistics Netherlands (CBS), see <www.internshipguide.elevenpub.com>*)

Each sector is composed of various industries. This is not the place to mention all of them, so here's a sector with its associated industries to serve as an example:

J   *Information and communication*
58 Publishing
59 Motion picture and television programme production and distribution; sound recording and music publishing
60 Programming and broadcasting
61 Telecommunications
62 Support activities in the field of information technology
63 Information service activities

The numbers are used by the Dutch Chamber of Commerce for the classification of the Trade Register. Here's another sector, related to the one above:

M   *Consultancy, research, and other specialized business services*
69 Legal services, accounting, tax consultancy, administration
70 Holding companies (not financial), support activities for the own enterprise group, and management and business consultancy
71 Architects, engineers, and technical design and consultancy; testing and analysis
72 Research and development
73 Advertising and market research
74 Industrial design, photography, translation, and other consultancy
75 Veterinary activities

Veterinary service providers are therefore not part of the human health and social work activities sector. In order to illustrate how detailed the industry classification is, below you will find a further dissection of the Dutch publishing industry:

Subclassification of an industry into sub-industries

58   Publishing

58.1   Publishing of books, magazines, etc.

58.11   Book publishing

58.13   Publishing of newspapers

58.14   Publishing of journals and magazines

58.19   Other publishing (no software)

58.2   Software publishing

58.21   Publishing of computer games

58.29   Other software publishing

If you are interested in publishing and want to contact a publishing house, the information above tells you it's a good idea to first find out what it is they publish. Naturally, you should also find out what their publications are intended for (*e.g.* are they literary or educational?), and which field they cover (*e.g.* history, IT).

Lastly, an excellent example is the classification of the motion picture and television programme production and distribution industry. Mind you, the *broadcast* of these programmes belongs to a different industry.

Subclassification of an industry into sub-industries

59   Motion picture and television programme production and distribution; sound recording and music publishing

59.1   Motion picture and television programme production and distribution

59.11   Motion picture and television programme production

59.11.1 Motion picture production (not for television)

59.11.2 Television programme production

59.12   Support activities to motion picture and television programme production

59.13   Distribution of motion pictures and television programmes

59.14   Cinemas

59.2   Sound recording and music publishing

59.20   Sound recording and music publishing

What does a sector or industry tell you? Starting with sectors, initially, the choice of sector tells you something about the part of the business chain you are interested in. If you are interested in how things are made and what they are made of, you might prefer sectors such as manufacturing or mining and quarrying. If you are interested in the delivery and service of products, you might prefer sectors such as renting and leasing of tangible goods and other business support services.

Secondly, you can tell by the type of sector whether the organizations that constitute that sector are profit-making organizations or non-profit organizations.

Sectors such as education and public administration, public services and compulsory social security are composed mainly of non-profit organizations, while most organizations in sectors that are concerned with production, trade, or services are profit making. Thirdly, you might have a natural inclination to work outdoors. In that case, sectors such as culture, sports, and recreation or agriculture, forestry, and fishing are a more obvious choice than manufacturing or human health and social work activities. You might, in all these fields, already feel an inclination towards a particular sector.

Next, there are industries. As the example of the publishing industry shows, an industry provides a more detailed view inside a sector because it focuses on a specific product. Your familiarity with a particular industry can influence your choice. Perhaps you know an industry really well because you grew up in a family that ran its own business. If you spent a lot of time in your father's or aunt's furniture factory as a child, this experience may have sown the seeds of a preference for – or an aversion to – the industry sector.

However, you can also have a preference for or aversion to an industry without having been directly in contact with that industry in your youth. Your attitude to life, for instance, may play a decisive role. For example, environment-minded people may be specifically interested in the food industry because they are interested in the production of goods. Your hobbies, too, may determine your preference for a certain industry. If you like working with children, you might be interested in the primary education industry. And even though you may never have given the agriculture, forestry, and fishing sector a moment's thought, if you are a wine buff, the growing of beverage crops might be quite to your taste.

Last but not least, your preference is, of course, determined by your choice of study. If you are a student of Tropical Forestry, you will naturally have a preference for the forestry industry. If you are a student of Theatre Studies, it is only logical that you consider working in the culture, sports, and recreation sector, specifically in the arts industry. And if you are following a degree programme in small business management, a placement with a small or medium-sized business (SMB: small and medium-sized business) is a logical choice. After all, you can learn the most about entrepreneurship under the direct supervision of an independent entrepreneur.

3.1.2 From Industry to Personal Profile

From top to bottom, it is easy to see why certain industries comprise the companies that they do. But, the other way around, it sometimes takes a little bit more effort to recognize the industry that a particular company belongs to. It is recommended that you learn to recognize these structures when looking for a placement because they provide information about the organizations that businesses cooperate with and about the money flows that are involved. More importantly, they provide information about the corporate culture of a particular organization and the kind of people that work there.

Suppose you consider doing a placement with a particular company that makes valves; you first have to find out who it produces for; a company producing valves for aeroplanes has a different corporate culture from one producing valves for household appliances. A training institute providing follow-up training for teachers in primary education has an entirely different atmosphere and type of staff from a training institute for train conductors or bakers. These are the differences that can help you choose a placement provider.

We will briefly return to an example in Step 2, the personal profile of a result-driven communications expert:

> As a communications expert, I am good at analysing communication processes within organizations. I take pleasure in formulating projects that can contribute to the optimalization of communication within an organization. I am proficient in drawing up and monitoring plans, but always keep an eye on the people whom it concerns. My flexibility allows me to make adjustments according to their needs. I like exchanging ideas with them about the process, both in writing as well as orally. However, I make sure never to lose sight of the aim of the project; when I start something I like to round it off successfully.

Civil service is probably not the best place for him. Failing to round off projects before the self-imposed deadline because of bureaucratic obstacles would cause him a lot of stress. On the other hand, someone who likes to examine matters in greater depth and investigate details and backgrounds would not enjoy working in a commercial organization that requires employees to meet a daily sales quota. He would be frustrated by the lack of time to dwell on a particular question or evaluation.

Here's another example of a personal profile:

> As a lawyer, I am good at untangling complex court cases. I like to get down to the bottom of cases that pose more questions than answers to other people. My knowledge of case law helps me distinguish fact from interpretation. I take honour in reaching a well-balanced verdict, and I enjoy explaining my conclusions to others. I take pleasure in explaining my decisions on paper. In my work, I take a particular interest in disadvantaged individuals.

The person who drew up this profile could send it to a court, and perhaps it was also written with this particular industry in mind. However, a medical environment would be an equally excellent choice, as lawyers are also needed in the health care industry.

Your profile should not be a means to exclude any sectors in advance. After all, a personal profile that you draw up yourself will always be slightly biased. Try to avoid the obvious. When getting started with your preparations, cast your net as wide as possible. This way you will avoid the trodden paths, and you might very well end up in the most unexpected places.

> Marc enters the placement office. He studies International Politics, a degree programme that includes a compulsory placement module. He is allowed to undertake a placement with commercial organizations, government bodies, but also NGOs, as long as the placement has an international component and the level and length of the assignment meet the requirements of his Master's programme. He asks the placement coordinator about the possibilities. The latter points at the world map on the wall and says, 'There are many'. This does not really help Marc, and neither does 'The world lies at your feet'. As a student of International Politics he has to find his own placement, so the possibilities are indeed rather limitless. Once this has got through to Marc, the placement coordinator asks him a question in return: 'What kind of placement would you like to do?' Marc tells her that he's heard about the possibility of doing a placement at a Dutch embassy. Again, the question: 'What would you like to do there?' and 'Why are you interested in that type of organization?' Many things spring to mind, but Marc has to admit that he actually doesn't really know what kind of things you can do at an embassy. The placement coordinator asks him if there are any particular topics that he is interested in. Has he ever written a paper on a topic that intrigued him? This gets Marc talking. He tells her that, during his studies, he specialized primarily in safety issues. He was born in Israel and has been back there, and has written an essay on Hamas; he would actually like to go back to his country of birth to conduct research into the Hamas-Israel issue. Visibly relieved, he decides to focus his search on academic institutes in Israel. Now that he knows precisely what he is looking for, it takes him less than two months to find a research institute that offers him a placement position . . . in Tel Aviv.

Unlike thirty other students at his faculty, Marc didn't opt for a placement at an embassy, thus accentuating his profile even more. Instead of going for the beaten path, he chose a slightly more difficult route. He reached higher. This has provided him not only with a unique experience, but also with specialist knowledge that dovetails with his studies and personal profile. Moreover, he has improved his command of his mother tongue. With this placement on his CV, Marc shows future employers what sets him apart from the others. It increases his chances of finding a job that closely ties in with his knowledge and interests.

3.1.3   From Personal Profile to Corporate Culture

Your personal profile says something about your competences and interests. It can be used as a jumping board to an organization, from which you subsequently move down again to a small position within it. You are lucky if you succeed in finding a company that matches your interests in an industry that fits your profile. To continue with the example of Marc from the previous section: it's great that he found an organization in a country that interests him, in an industry that allows him to do what he loves most (*i.e.* research), but this is no guarantee for a satisfactory placement. The evaluation form that Marc completed shows that he did not always feel at ease among his colleagues: his supervisor did not always make clear what was expected of Marc, and he felt that his motives for working were different from those of his colleagues. In short, he did not really feel at home there.

How did this happen? The previous section has already mentioned the existence of corporate culture. For students on placement, corporate culture is an important phenomenon, but, unfortunately, also one that is hard to grasp. But what is it, exactly? Corporate culture is 'the common understanding among the members of a company with respect to that company's day-to-day activities'.

> Corporate culture is the entirety of written and unwritten rules that channel and shape the social interaction between the staff of the company, as well as between the staff and third parties.
> *(Sanders and Nuijen, 1992)*

In contrast to what the term 'corporate culture' implies, the definition also includes non-profit organizations. Government bodies, too, all have a corporate culture of their own. As mentioned in the definition, a large part of that culture is unwritten, so it is hard to form a clear picture of a corporate culture of a company without having worked there. You could read their annual reports, newsletters, or website, but a large part will still remain hidden.

The perfect way to find out about an organization's culture is to speak to its employees. When talking about their work, employees often 'breathe' their corporate culture; you have to read between the lines to find out about the ways of the organization, about what is tolerated and what is not. You will have to listen to what someone tells you, but you should also pay attention to the signals they send out, because people will not readily say negative things about their own job. However, you could also try to figure out what values characterize an organization by means of fictional cases. You could then check whether these values match the career values you collected in Step 2.

3.1.4 The Position

As discussed in Step 2, apart from sectors, industries, and organizations, you can, of course, also base your choice on the kind of position you want to hold. What are your ambitions? Do you have minimum and maximum demands? Do you want to work full-time or part-time? Would you be interested in a job at the placement-providing organization?

You should know that your answers to the questions above indicate the degree to which you consider your placement to be a serious step in your career. Perhaps you want your placement to be a fun experience more than anything else, or you just want to undertake a placement in the capital of Mexico at the same time as your best friend.

If you are interested in a position in business (*i.e.* the profit-making sector) and you want to increase your chances of receiving a job offer after the placement, it's wise to undertake a placement with a larger company. Small businesses often have a need for students on placement, but chances that a position becomes available exactly at the time that you are rounding off your placement are smaller than at a company that has multiple departments or branches. This is because smaller businesses have less mobility. Also, the specialized nature of a small business makes it less likely that they have job vacancies that exactly match your degree programme and profile.

In order to find out whether a position within a certain organization requires you to work many hours and what the chances are of a position opening up, the best thing to do is to make an appointment with someone who works there. Once you have told them that you are interested in the organization and that you would like to know more about the work that it is involved in, an employee of the department relevant to your interests may be willing to talk to you. You can easily do this by telephone, but in some cases it is customary to suggest having lunch together. This is the case at institutions of the European Union in Brussels or Strasbourg, for instance. This way, you show them that you are genuinely interested, and it gives you time to prepare questions about their work.

You might find out, for example, that a project leader for an educational publisher usually works in the evenings because those are the only moments he gets to speak to his authors. After all, many authors work as teachers or lecturers during the day and write textbooks in the evening as an additional activity. Or you might find out that a placement with a documentary programme is not nearly as interesting as you thought because the production of a documentary takes six months, and the maker is a freelance filmmaker who schedules the intakes and shooting days from his home, possibly with the help of a production assistant of the broadcasting company. This means that you will not be able to experience both the pre-production and the post-production of the broadcast (that is, if the placement period is shorter than the time it takes to make the documentary), and that there is no proper workplace where you can work together with an editorial staff.

3.1.5   The Placement Assignment

Once you know how to describe yourself (in a personal profile), which industry you are interested in, and which career values are important to you, it is time to focus on the placement assignment. The placement assignment – the actual work you will be doing – is what you ultimately base your choice of placement on.

Perhaps you think that the assignment will be drawn up by the host institution. This is indeed the case with placement vacancies, or projects that have to be carried out in addition to the fixed tasks, like organizing a conference or festive event. In these cases, the host institution has no choice but to explain in broad terms what is to be done. Remarkably often, however, placement providers do not have a clearly defined assignment ready, simply because they are not used to dealing with small sub-assignments, or because they have not yet taken the time to think of any tasks that students could carry out within a short time frame. They just don't know what a placement should involve according to your degree programme.

You therefore face the challenging task of deciding on a possible job description before you can start applying for a placement. However, you will often have no idea what exactly a placement entails. But how do you find out? How do you get an answer to the question 'What would you like to do in our organization?'

One possibility is to approach fellow students who have done a placement and ask them about their assignment. Perhaps your degree programme provides placement reports of others for you to read. These are often publicly available. You could also visit placement vacancy websites to search for assignment descriptions of placements that match your study programme.

One thing you should definitely do is find out about the criteria lecturers use in assessing placement assignments. A recent survey among 515 students at five different universities of applied sciences revealed that, at the start of their place-ment, only 36% were aware of the requirements they had to meet in order to suc-cessfully complete the placement assignment. To the question 'Was it clear to you in advance what requirements you had to meet in order to complete the assignment successfully?', 14% replied 'No, not at all', and 50% 'Just a little' (Lampe et al., 2009). This is, of course, a little bit strange, to put it mildly . . .

Most degree programmes do actually have a manual or website listing the formal requirements of a placement (as described in an example in Step 1). Your lecturer can also give you examples of assignments that qualify for your degree programme and those that do not. This is important information, as you can only start your placement once the assignment has been approved by the lecturer.

Examples of placement assignments of university students in the Netherlands

An assignment at the Bachelor's degree level:
A student of Journalism and New Media is doing a placement with the web edi-torial board of a Dutch broadcasting company. The assignment: to find out how visitors use the website and to identify what improvements can be made to its design, user-friendliness, and content. This will result in a recommendation re-port that can be used as a starting point for the development of a new website.

An assignment at the Master's degree level:
A student of International Management is doing a placement with a consul-tancy that advises and assists Dutch entrepreneurs who want to do business with East African entrepreneurs and vice versa. The assignment: to support an incoming trade mission from Ethiopia to the Netherlands in the field of tourism. His tasks are, among other things, to recruit businesses, to match Dutch entre-preneurs with Ethiopian entrepreneurs, and to organize the trade mission itself. In addition to the placement report, the assignment will also result in a strategy for organizing trade missions.

Examples of placement assignments of university students abroad

An assignment at the Bachelor's degree level:
A History student is doing a placement at a French embassy. The assignment: to investigate the extent to which the French business community has benefited from an agreement made by the European Union. This investigation will result in a report that discusses per sector which economic opportunities have been taken advantage of and which ones can still be benefited from by the French business community in that area.

An assignment at the Master's degree level:

A student of Humanitarian Assistance is doing a placement with an NGO that provides international aid to elderly people, and sets off for the branch in the Caribbean. The assignment: to set up a project that aims to prepare elderly people in Jamaica better for a disaster or crisis. This will result in a project plan that gives a detailed description of the project's aims, activities, and budget. In addition, she will conduct a survey among elderly people to find out about their current situation as far as natural disasters are concerned, and will report on this. Finally, she will write a handbook on the social protection of the elderly in that area.

Once you have collected examples of placement assignment descriptions that tie in with your degree programme, you of course still need to make a choice. At this point, you still have time to decide which assignments do and do not appeal to you. The selection you end up with may cause a shift in the selection of organizations you made earlier. It is possible that you chose literary publisher as your preferred type of organization, while the assignment type that appeals to you – say, organizing a congress – does not tie in with that organization at all. To succeed, you have to match your preferred type of organization with your preferred type of assignment.

3.2   Placement Advertisements

It may come as a surprise, but matching yourself with an organization is actually not that big a step. The challenge has been to find a placement with an organization that gives you the opportunity to make the most of the talents you described. You already highlighted in the previous steps the elements that play a role in this: your profile, the sector, the industry, the corporate culture, and potential placement assignments.

You managed to influence some factors slightly, but not all. There are also factors that you could not have foreseen. Something to help you in your search for placement vacancies is placement advertisements. The best source for these is the Internet. Your search should not be limited to the vacancy websites that pop up when you google 'placement vacancy'; many organizations advertise current vacancies on their website, and these can't always be found in placement databases.

You can use placement advertisements to compare your personal profile with the profiles that companies use in their job descriptions; the so-called *job-related competency profiles*. For example, Amsterdam's city borough 'Amsterdam-

Noord' announced a vacancy for Head of Department of Businesses and Real Estate. The advertisement described the job-related competency profile for the new manager as 'a mix of attitude features, skills, personality traits, and competencies. This mix reveals a clear underlying competency profile, which we use for selection interviews and can be used in assessments! The advertisement first lists a number of core competencies that apply to all of the borough's personnel:

- *'Cooperation*: works together with others in order to achieve team goals; shares information with others, and supports others.
- *Awareness of the people around you*: has an eye, care, and respect for the feelings of others; shows an interest in other people's opinions; displays a positive and tolerant attitude towards differences in needs and views.
- *Result-driven*: carries out projects smoothly; achieves results; makes sure that important goals are attained.
- *Customer-oriented*: aims to provide smooth, efficient, and personal service to customers; does everything in his or her power to satisfy the customer's needs!

The job-related competencies of the new Head of Department are:

- *'Analytical ability*: distinguishes between main aspects and related aspects; can break down a complex question into components and establishes logical connections between the different elements.
- *Organizational awareness*: identifies organizational political processes and understands the working procedures within an organization.
- *Coaching*: supervises employees in their tasks and stimulates their personal development.
- *Guidance*: manages people and processes while monitoring progress.
- *Initiative*: takes action independently; identifies chances and opportunities and responds to them; is proactive.
- *Business acumen:* is aware of financial matters and business matters; focuses on costs, profits, markets, new business opportunities, and on activities that yield the highest return!

Compare your personal profile with an advertisement and you will see that the differences between types of competence can be traced back to the subject-specific and generic competencies discussed in Step 2.

Janet wants to undertake a work placement. She's in luck: she has found a placement vacancy that appeals to her. However, she still has doubts because the advertisement states that students who apply for the placement have to be 'proactive! This raises some questions: how can she find out if she is proactive? She has never been on placement before and has never had a job that ties in with her degree programme. How can she possibly know if she would take the initiative under such circumstances? Can't she only know this in hindsight? It

is almost funny how this requirement not only amazes her, but almost annoys her, too; there appears to be some anger in her voice. The placement coordinator, who has never spoken to Janet before, welcomes her frankness. By asking all these questions, Janet has – unknowingly – provided the answer herself. She has, after all, taken the initiative to meet with the placement coordinator, she has started asking the questions (instead of the fellow student whom she came with), and she is not afraid to open herself up. The answer to her question is simple: how does she behave among a group of friends? For instance, what does she do when they decide to eat out together? Does she arrange the date? Does she call the restaurant? And what did she do in her part-time job when, for instance, something was out of stock? Did she report this? Did she place an order? Janet answers all these questions with a nod. She can start applying for the placement; she is proactive and matches the profile described in the advertisement.

You should be aware, however, that only 16% of placements are found through advertisements. All other placements are found by word of mouth or through unsolicited applications. However, having a look at advertisements gives you a better idea of what you are looking for. You can then also start sending unsolicited applications to organizations, something that networking can really help you with.

Conclusion

This step described how you can perform a market analysis. In other words, it explained how to find an organization that can offer you a placement assignment
that dovetails with the personal profile you drew up in Step 2. This chapter showed
you what sectors are distinguished by the Chamber of Commerce, and also gave a
number of examples of industries and sub-industries that belong to those sectors.
These overviews provide information on the cash flows between organizations and
enable you to identify them as commercial organizations or non-profit organizations. The distinction between commercial and non-profit gives you information
about the *culture* within an organization. By comparing this information to your
personal profile, you can find out the kind of organization you belong to. Once you
have found a suitable organization, you can focus on potential positions, which, in
their turn, belong to different departments within that organization. As a result, the
placement assignment that you agree on in the end will be as close as possible to the
kind of job that appeals to you the most.

Step 4 Networking

As you have seen in Step 3, there are different ways to find out what the labour market has to offer; you can get information from the Internet, lectures, business days, workshops and open days, written information, and personal information. Of all of these sources, personal information is the most valuable. Personal contact can do what a website, a workshop, or a brochure cannot. A pleasant personal interview, however brief, can open the doors to the placement of your dreams. This whole chapter is therefore dedicated to obtaining personal information, but it will also show you how the other sources of information can play a role.

4.1   What Is Networking?

Networking means that you search for a placement or job with the help of people you know. Networking is 'making and maintaining contacts'. Through networking, you collect information, advice, and new contacts. Networking comes naturally to people. Think of a student looking for his first room; apart from searching through advertisements on real and online notice boards and newspapers, he will also ask people he knows for information. If they can't help him, he will ask them if they know anyone who can. He will write down the names and telephone numbers and contact his acquaintances' friends shortly after. On the phone, he will probably refer to their mutual acquaintance: 'Your name was given to me by . . . ' This way, the other person will be more willing to cooperate, which makes it easier to find a room.

Networking for a placement is similar to networking for a room. The difference is, of course, that when you network for a placement you do not offer money in return (as you do for a room), but your qualities. You should have a clear idea of what they are, and be convinced that you are able and willing to use those qualities in your placement.

The word 'networking' has a negative connotation for some people. To them, the word sounds cold and calculating, perhaps because it reminds them of the sometimes negatively interpreted term 'connections', which is associated with finding a job with the help of other people's contacts – while it is actually not all that bad if you say you have found a placement by word of mouth. Also, your friends are part of your network too, as are family, fellow students, and neighbours. Incidentally, the way people network often differs from culture to culture.

Another name for this step could have been 'asking people you know for advice' instead of 'networking' if it did not sound so one-sided. After all, networking is not just benefiting from the information and contacts of others; networking is primarily *reciprocal* in character – or, as experienced networkers put it, networking is 'taking and giving'. 'Taking' refers to the information you are looking for, and in return you 'give' your network contacts something that they are interested in. This could be anything: a tip about an interesting article that was recently published, the name of your lecturer who specializes in a particular field, the perfect restaurant for delicious Italian food, or . . . your competences that are ideally suited for the placement in question!

4.2   Networking vs. Applying for a Placement

Networking is *not* the same as applying for a job or placement. Networking is talking to people you know, acquaintances of people you know, and people you don't know. Asking a person for a placement or job straightaway will not get you anywhere – not only because that person would get the feeling that he or she is just a means to achieving your goal (instead of a person with qualities), but also because you are asking for the impossible. Individual employees simply do not have placements and jobs lying around for you. The only thing they might have is *information about* possible opportunities or *contacts* who might be able to help you.

The goal of a networking conversation is therefore always to *ask for advice*. Almost everyone appreciates being called on for their expertise. If you ask someone to meet up with you to tell you more about a subject that you expect them to know much about, they will rarely say no. Therefore, unlike job interviews, a networking conversation requires you to prepare a clearly formulated question, which will give you some information on placements or jobs within the organization concerned. The advice you are asking for may concern a particular sector of the labour market, a particular position (or the tasks it involves), or, for instance, the content of a project. You are expected to first find out as much as possible for yourself, though. Section 4.4 describes the steps that you can take in order to come to a request for advice.

Networking for a placement is done step by step. You have to work in circles, as it were. With the help of people you know, and then with the help of acquaintances of the people you know, and later on in the process sometimes also with the help of strangers, you gradually get closer to the placement you are looking for. Perhaps you have gone no further than the first step and already know which organization you are looking for – as is the case with job interviews – but you may also be 'circling' more than one company or institution. This is what makes networking more exciting than applying for a placement. You have to try to get to speak to the right people to get your questions answered – and again, *do not ask for work!*

Many people who embraced networking enjoy the excitement. After all, you always make an appointment with someone you 'feel connected to' in a way; you pick them for a reason: they possess knowledge that you are looking for. You have something in common with them: you share an interest, are involved in the same professional fields, or encounter the same kinds of problems. Many networking conversations are therefore inspiring experiences that often reveal something unexpected. For that reason, you never know exactly what step you will want to take after such a conversation. Also, an inspiring conversation like that may unexpectedly turn out to be the first one of many.

In that sense, networking is more *active* than applying. You know what you are really good at and what kind of work you are looking for, and this is what you tell the people whom you make an appointment with. You are therefore in control, more so than when applying for a placement. In the case of application procedures, the employers are the ones who clearly and prominently profile themselves in the market. As soon as they advertise a vacancy, you write a letter in order to be considered for the job. Once you have done that, the only thing you can do is wait and see whether you have been selected: a time-consuming and sometimes frustrating activity, especially when you are turned down, which will always put a little dent in your self-esteem. Networking is less asymmetrical. The employer is not the only one in command. Moreover, because you are the initiator, you have a big say in the topic of conversation.

By having a grip on the agenda, you can better influence the image that people form of you. This is a nice feeling, which in turn leads to your being able to demonstrate a more relaxed attitude during the conversation. Also, networking is often more fun than applying for a job or placement. It boosts your self-esteem and teaches you a great deal about types of work, types of organization, sectors, and the labour market as a whole. In addition, the actual application process will often turn out to be easier if you have been networking. You will write better letters and will present yourself more easily during job interviews, especially because you have a better idea of what you can do and what you want to do than before you started networking, which makes you radiate self-awareness.

Is this the way to find a placement, by just talking to people?

> Experience shows that, yes, most of the time it is. Especially when you show enough patience and perseverance, the moment will come that the step towards writing an application (unsolicited or not) will speak for itself. Or, even better, that you will be asked to apply. (Van Eeden, 2004: 35)

You can, of course, apply for placements alongside your networking activities, if only because it gives you the opportunity to practice your interview skills and writing application letters and CVs. After all, you would be crazy not to respond to an attractive vacancy.

Do add networking to your search because it will triple your chances. Advertising is not only a time-consuming and expensive activity for companies, but they also prefer to rely on their own network to recruit people. Many placement vacancies, especially those found on the Internet, are outdated because they have already been filled. Government bodies in some countries are required by law to recruit externally for every position, which is why they sometimes place advertisements for positions that have already been filled internally. Commercial companies often use job advertisements to advertise their success, thus using vacancies as advertising material. These vacancies do not exist in reality or have already been filled and are kept in the media for a little longer for publicity's sake.

Even as a second-year Bachelor's student of History, Maurice knew where he wanted to do his placement. Fascinated with everything United Nations (UN)-related, his dream was to work with the Permanent Representation of the Netherlands at the UN in New York. When he heard that his fellow student Laura was doing a placement there, he decided to look her up. He booked a ticket to New York and asked her countless questions about her work. He had carefully planned the moment of his visit; through his e-mail correspondence with Laura, he had learned that the Dutch ambassador would be organizing a drinks reception in the first week of April to which all Dutch people of the UN Security Council had been invited. Laura wrote to Maurice that if he scheduled his New York visit in that particular week, he could accompany her to the reception. It all worked out. Not only did the reception give Maurice the chance to shake hands with the ambassador's, but he also managed – as he had planned – to get in touch with the man responsible for arranging work placements through the Ministry of Foreign Affairs in The Hague. Four months later, Maurice mentioned his visit to New York in his application letter. His letter was one of four that were selected from a total of twenty-seven letters, and he was invited for a job interview in The Hague. The moment he entered the room he already knew that his networking conversation would probably be a success: the man at the other end of the table was the same man he had spoken to at the drinks reception in New York. Maurice reminded the man of their meeting in the United States and . . . was accepted for the placement. There was simply no student more motivated than him.

The most important reason why you should network is that it allows you to search more specifically than if you were to limit yourself to placement vacancies only. Many placement opportunities are 'hidden'. For example, an organization may be faced with an extra workload during a particular period but it does not warrant hiring an extra employee. The work still needs to be done, though, and it might not have occurred to the manager to take on a student on placement.

A company may have a variety of tasks lying around for years without anyone taking responsibility for them. As a student on placement, an ideal assignment for you might be to examine these tasks (as a social scientist), to put these tasks into a certain perspective (as a management expert), or to carry them out (as a facility manager). Another example might be an organization that may have an annually recurring project that requires a new theme each year. The open-minded approach of a student on placement may ensure a fresh new image year after year. As these examples show, placement assignments are often project-based, and capturing their essence in a straightforward job description is not always possible. However, if you get the chance to tell someone you're networking with what you would like to do, you are bound to find tasks like these. You might never find such placement opportunities if you limit your search to vacancies only.

4.3   Networking Is 'Giving' Something

You cannot network if you have nothing to offer.

> 'A good networker is someone who has the guts to step up to people, who can bring people in contact with each other, who knows what he or she wants to achieve, and whose intentions are clear' is what a politician once said in an interview. She attends symposia, grass-roots meetings, dinners, and hospitals for her portfolios Health Care and Youth and Families. Networking is a daily activity for her, and in the care sector she knows people from the very top to the nurses working at the bedside. She used to go into meetings having no idea whom she would be speaking to, but nowadays she comes prepared: she is more focused now and knows which people will be there and whom she wants to speak to. Her advice: 'make sure you have something to say or ask when you walk up to someone.'

What do you need to be able to network properly? First, you need to have an *interest* in people. This need not be difficult because you only need to take an interest in people who may provide useful information. And, yes, this is indeed a case of circular reasoning that always holds true.

You cannot show an interest in someone without gathering information first; you need to learn about the people you want to approach by finding out what their position entails and what their interests are, but also by acquainting yourself with and relating to their culture. There are major differences between nationalities and they manifest themselves in minor incidents. These cultural differences may also manifest themselves between European countries, and they can work against you, especially at moments when you least expect it.

Secondly, you need a clear *aim*. If done properly, the personal profile you drew up in Step 2 (Self-Analysis) describes your aim clearly. You have thought about what you want and what you are looking for.

Next, you should make sure that your aim is *formulated clearly*. It would be absurd to recite your entire personal profile to your friend's father at her party because he shows an interest. A much more practical approach is to prepare an 'elevator pitch'. Networking conversations may sometimes take place at unexpected moments, so you always need to have a pitch ready. An elevator pitch is a presentation of approximately one minute (one hundred to two hundred words) in which you recommend yourself. It sounds awful, but it is not. Preparing for an elevator pitch forces you to summarize your personal profile. In a couple of sentences you explain enthusiastically who you are and what you are good at. You can use terms from the STAR Method (see Section 6.1.3) and from your profile sketch (see Section 3.1.2 and further) for this purpose. Try to

keep your elevator pitch a little flexible; you use it to show someone you are interested in that *you* are the perfect solution to their problem.

> Sophie is on her way to a networking appointment at a company she is interested in. She happens to know the manager because she has already spoken to him via her father. Coincidentally, the manager steps into the elevator with her. He recognizes her, greets her kindly, and asks her what she is doing here. 'I have an appointment with Nico de Vries. I am looking for a placement.' The manager nods, appearing interested, and asks her what kind of placement she is looking for. The question takes Sophie by surprise. All she can bring herself to say is, 'Something to do with communication.' The manager nods, the elevator stops, and Sophie missed out on a golden opportunity. If she'd had her elevator pitch ready, she would have been able to pitch her dream placement within the minute it takes to ride the elevator. She would have told him that she is doing the specialization in Internal Communication as part of the Communication Science programme, and is interested in a placement concerning the internal distribution of management information. The manager has just established a working group for the development of an organization-wide intranet. Her elevator pitch could have given him the idea to offer her a placement position to help out with this project.

There is no denying that networking also requires a bit of *courage*: courage to call someone who was recommended to you by someone else, courage to ask that person if they have time to meet, and, once you have made an appointment, courage to adopt a vulnerable attitude. You also need courage to say that you need advice. Finally, you need the courage to tell them your ideas about a subject that fascinates you and the courage to accept their feedback.

Apart from courage, you will also need *patience* and *perseverance*. After all, only one out of five phone calls leads to an appointment with the right person.

> Benno is an experienced networker. He works as a management consultant for SMBs in his area. He acquires many of his jobs by phone. " I usually need to call over and over again in order to get a new contact on the phone; I can't let my voice reflect my boredom, though. When I call a company for the first time, I usually get to speak to a secretary first. I tell her my name and whom I'm calling for, and she tries to put me through. Four times out of five, the person I want to speak to is 'not at his desk'. I then ask her when he can be reached later in the day and tell her I'll call back. I then note down the time in my diary because I've noticed that people think you are more reliable if you call back at the specified time. If the person you want to speak to is unavailable at the specified time, the secretary might feel guilty and will likely offer to help. Often, she will ask you what you're calling for. I rarely fall for this. A secretary can't always judge how important a subject is to the person I wish to speak to. I then tell her that I want to discuss something that may be of a lot of interest to that person, and that I'd rather explain it to him myself. She can still help me, at best by giving me his mobile phone number – I guard mobile phone numbers like a treasure. At the very least, she can promise me that I'll be called back. In that case, I make sure that I can be easily reached and that I have the right question ready for *if* he calls – which, by the way, seldom happens . . ."

Perhaps you are under the impression that you need to establish a large network in order to be able to network properly. This is not true: your family, fellow students, lecturers, sports buddies, and neighbours form the basis of your network and this basis easily consists of 250 people. You won't find all of them in your address book, but they form the basis that can help you get in contact with *anyone*. Do you need to? Probably not, but it does show you that your dream placement is within reach if you have an interest in people, a clear aim, a clear story, and some courage and perseverance.

Finally, it is important to point out that, above all, networking means *listening*. When chattering away enthusiastically you might forget to pay attention to how the other person reacts, while it is so important to identify the other person's needs and to meet those needs as much as possible. Is your contact person interested mainly in the theoretical side? Does he ask you about the latest professional literature in your field? This means it is a good idea to discuss your research skills and study skills and how they can be applied to a placement assignment. If, on the other hand, your contact person is interested mainly in the practical side, you can tell him about the activities you organized outside your degree programme. If the contact person wants to pass your profile to someone else, offer to send him your CV and add a little note with a summary of your personal profile and a thank-you for the conversation.

4.4   Networking Is 'Taking' Something

If you want to network for a nice placement, your first goal is to gain something from it. You of course offer knowledge, competences, and motivation in return, but the person you are speaking with will not always have a direct use for those. For example, they might not need a student on placement themselves, but do know someone who can help you. Prior to a conversation, you may not exactly know what you can 'give'. You should therefore first focus on your request for advice; in other words, on what you want to 'take'.

Networking with a particular purpose in mind is a time-consuming activity. Sometimes you have subconsciously been looking for conversational links that might lead to a placement, sometimes you have been doing this very consciously. This chapter discusses the conscious approach, which you can use to learn how to network. By following this method, you can develop networking into a 'second nature', as it were. It is like learning to ride a bicycle: if, in the future, you are looking for a job (or something else), you will only have to brush up on the networking skills you are acquiring now and use them again when you need to – by focusing on social media, for example.

4.4.1   Functional Résumé

Assuming you have already drawn up a personal profile (Step 2), you have already completed a major part of your preparations. Your personal profile describes who you are, but it does not state the aim of your networking conversations. Therefore, when you start networking, you supplement your personal profile with a 'functional résumé'.

A functional résumé is the key document for networking. Unlike a CV (see Step 5), this document looks *ahead*. It describes your profile (your knowledge and abilities) plus the kind of work you are looking for. It describes your work and study experience in such a way that your aim is the next logical step.

Initially, the functional résumé is only for personal use (Van Eeden, 2004: 34). It is, as it were, your focal point, the focus you remind yourself of in every conversation. In that way, it is also the agenda in all your conversations. Since you enter every networking conversation with a clear aim in mind, you have a greater chance of success – so do not immediately send it out to everyone.

Add a *request for advice* to the aim stated in your functional résumé, and put this on paper in advance. Once you have prepared your aim and your request for advice, you can start your 'networking campaign'.

> Eric wants to do a placement. He is exploring the possibilities and has a number of starting points. First, he wants to do a placement that will improve his English – he's a student of American Studies, so that would be very useful. Moreover, he reasons that it would be easier for him to improve his English this way than by following an extra language course (which would involve the necessary studying). Eric's first idea is therefore to go abroad. Secondly, he wants it to be a paid placement. As he is no longer entitled to a student grant, he cannot practically undertake a placement without remuneration. He has to look for a placement provider who is willing to pay him more than €500 net per month. This is going to make things difficult for him; the content of the placement is far more important to him. He has two possible themes in mind: microcredit and accountable governance. Until recently, Eric worked at a large bank to finance his studies. His job there involved microfinance, which taught him a lot about the subject. He noticed that the banking world pays little attention to microcredit, and wishes to undertake a placement in order to delve into the subject more deeply. Unfortunately, he lost his job due to the financial crisis in 2008. This also means that he lost the opportunity to do a placement there. He decides to look for a placement in the United States because it fits in with his degree programme and his wish to improve his English. As a subject, he decides to opt for microcredit because his chances of getting remuneration in that field are higher than in accountable governance. He writes a summary of his CV and adds the following aim: 'I am looking for a paid placement with a commercial institution in The United States of America that provides microcredit.'

74

4.4.2   The First Circle: The People You Know

Networking brings you closer to your dream placement. You will conduct the first networking conversations with people close to you, but do make sure they are people who can bring you closer to your goal. Consider, for example, members of your family you don't often get to speak to (*e.g.* the uncle who, for his business, moved abroad a few years ago) or a good friend or fellow student.

Close acquaintances themselves also have a circle of people around them, and you won't know most of them. It's an easy sum, really: when you have 50 close acquaintances who all have 50 close acquaintances themselves, you easily have $50 \times 50 = 2{,}500$ people within your reach.

You start with people who already know you, so the threshold for making an appointment will not be that high. However, do make sure that your conversation is about your functional résumé, and do not hide away your question in a friendly visit to the pub or cinema. Networking with acquaintances not only helps you to get advice on a placement, but also allows you to practise these kind of conversations. You can ask a friend or family member if your aim is feasible, if it fits your experience, and what they think of the way you present your goal.

Hannah started a secretarial course after gaining her secondary school diploma. The course allowed her to work two days a week. The combination of learning and working gave her a sense of independence. Almost immediately after completing the secretarial course, she was hired as a municipal government office manager. The company received frequent visits from a group of Finns because of an education partnership with Helsinki; it was Hannah's job to organize and supervise these visits. The Finnish language fascinated Hannah, and the visits made her curious about the language. She decided to pursue a Bachelor's degree programme in Finno-Ugric Languages and Cultures. She decided to take a break from work in her third year of study; she preferred to combine work and study by means of a placement instead. She explained this to her father, who suggested that she accompany him to a drinks party at the international company he works at. There, she spoke to a man who worked at the branch in Finland but who regularly attended the office in the Netherlands as well. She asked him about the possibilities of doing a placement at the Finnish branch for someone with her profile. She told him that she was fluent in Finnish, but that she wished to improve her language skills even further by using it in daily life. The man invited her to apply for a placement as a secretarial assistant in Finland. Hannah managed to persuade her lecturer to give his approval. The fact that she had to prepare notes in Finnish as well as speak Finnish daily on the phone and in meetings made this placement suitable for the Finno-Ugric Bachelor's degree programme.

You can use the answer to your request for advice to refine your functional résumé. Your aim will become more and more concrete with every conversation not only because you will learn how best to present your aim but also because every conversation gives you more information on how to achieve that aim.

4.4.3   The Second Circle: Acquaintances of People You Know

Acquaintances won't hesitate to put you in touch with their friends or colleagues. Most acquaintances will enjoy being able to help you on your way and won't mind it if you pass on their name to the person they refer you to. But make no mistake: you are networking, and the essence of networking is *trust*. Why is it that employers rather employ, or in any other way cooperate with someone they know by word of mouth? Because everyone would rather work with someone they know, someone from whom they know what to expect. Networking is a way to achieve this and to rule out any nasty surprises or disappointments as much as possible.

You should therefore always agree very clearly on how to contact the person they recommend to you – even if it is your sister or mother you are networking with. Do they want you to get in touch with their acquaintance directly and to mention them as the one who referred you to that person, or would they rather call their acquaintance themselves to say that you will be getting in touch with them? Whichever is the case, do not wait too long with arranging your second networking appointment. You are networking, so you want to leave a serious impression on all your networking partners.

You'll find it less easy to make an appointment with people from the second circle because you don't know them as well as you do your friends and family. It is important, however, *not to wait too long*; your first contact might already have tipped off their networking contact, and he or she will be waiting for your phone call.

> Example: 'My sister told me that you worked for Ahold until recently. Can you please tell me how to approach that company for a placement with their marketing department?'

People in the second circle are actually hardest to network with. After all, you have to work on the basis of the impression that the person from the first circle has given of you and of the person you are contacting. Assume as neutral a position as possible, have a clear question ready, and always pass on the outcome of the conversation to the person who brought you two in contact with each other.

4.4.4   The Third Circle: Everyone!

When the person from the second circle refers you to someone you don't know at all, you have reached the *third circle*. Naturally, this is a very large circle becausee it comprises everyone you don't know. Section 4.4.2 mentioned that

50 acquaintances can bring you into direct contact with 2,500 people. In their turn, these 2,500 people can, via *their* acquaintances, come into contact with 2,500 people in their second circle. This easily amounts to 2,500 × 2,500 = more than 6 million people. There may be overlap here as well, but let's assume for now that 4 million of these contacts are unique.

> I never knew that my friend Michael shook Bill Clinton's hand – not until he gave me a tour of his house and we arrived in the study where I saw a photo of them together. They were looking into the camera, smiling: Bill with a routine smile on his face, Michael looking slightly flabbergasted. Naturally, I asked him why this photo was taken, and it turned out it had happened by chance. Michael met Bill while the former president was out on a jog during a visit to England; Michael had picked up the courage to ask for a handshake and a photo.
>
> This immediately reminded me of the three handshakes theory. Don't they say that everyone on Earth is no more than three handshakes away from Bill Clinton? That's only one handshake for me now; the only one still standing between Bill and me is my friend Michael. I start thinking about the massive increase in my network after this discovery: from now on, I'm only two handshakes away from all the great names: both George Bushes, Al Gore, Obama, Hillary, Queen Elizabeth, and, last but not least, Nelson Mandela.
>
> (Source: <www.loopbaanadvies.net>, blog, 6 August 2009)

Getting in touch with someone famous is interesting only if that individual is the sole person who can answer your question; however, information about celebrities can help you in another way. Take the example of Eric in Section 4.4.1: he wanted to undertake a placement in the field of microcredit. When planning networking meetings, it's important that he keeps track of the developments in microcredit, not only those in the Netherlands, but especially those in the United States. Chances are that he frequently stumbles across the name of the Dutch princess Máxima. She has been involved in microcredit for years, and it is possible that funds have been generated in her name to provide people with microcredit. These funds need to be managed, and the institutions responsible for such management need students on placement.

To some people this may sound like a flight of fancy – something very unlikely to happen. However, the core of the matter is that you won't get any further by carrying out networking conversations *alone*. As discussed in Section 4.4.3, the focus that is needed to leave a good impression – even if it concerns your mother – is also needed when dealing with all the information that is coming your way. You will have to read the newspaper every day, keep track of specialist literature, attend lectures on your favourite subjects, and keep up to date on the latest news on radio, TV, and the Internet.

You are probably aware that news is characterized by *hypes*. If there have been fires in multiple student flats in your student city, you can bet your life on it that the university paper will write an article on what to do in case of fire. The board of the university will then demand that a disaster contingency plan is drawn up, the deputy mayor will order the fire department to pay every student flat in the city a preventive visit, and the International Housing Office will publish an information brochure for foreign students.

Similar hypes are apparent in the way that money is spent in some countries. When reading between the lines, you often learn more about the news than what the news item itself is telling you. While 'innovation' used to be the buzzword in the business world, these days (2012) it is all about 'sustainability' – years ago, that term would have made people ridicule you at networking events, calling you a 'tree hugger'.

The third circle of your network does not know you, so the way you present yourself should correspond to your aim and profile. Tell people in your third circle that you would like some advice, and let them know that *you know what is going on in the sector in question*. After all, you have been following the news and reading information about the company. Mention, for instance, a current project that interests you. It shows that you respect your networking partner and that you are serious about achieving your aim. You could send them your functional résumé or CV in advance if they ask for this. Do emphasize that the main reason you are calling is that you have a *question*, though; in order to prepare for a placement, you need information about a particular subject: about the sector, the organization, or the job characteristics of a particular profession.

Trying to achieve your goal this way (using that necessary bit of courage) can lead to unexpected encounters. If you ask students who found a placement this way how exactly they got their hands on a placement position, they will tell you that it happened by chance. What they do not realize is that they themselves created opportunities, which they could then seize with both hands.

> Paul wants to do a placement for his Master's degree programme in History. He is rounding off his thesis and would now like to gain some practical experience. Thanks to a friend, he gets to send an unsolicited application to an employee at the Ministry of Education, Culture, and Science. This results in a 1-hour interview. The employee writes a short report about the interview and e-mails it to a colleague because he knows that she is involved in the organization of an exhibition of National Archives material. This material has not yet been widely on display, and it could be said that it is, in fact, somewhat 'forgotten'. The Ministry employee suspects that his colleague could use a young student on placement with a fresh approach to present the material attractively to the public. Paul wonders how to prepare for the second interview. How will he know

> if the placement assignment at the National Archives fits in with his degree pro-
> gramme? The placement coordinator advises him to prepare for this interview
> as if it were an official application. He may be asked to name his best and worst
> qualities, or to give examples of, for instance, his 'perseverance'. He then refers
> Paul to the supervising lecturer of the History department. It would be useful
> to discuss the emphasis of the assignment with her: should the emphasis be
> on helping out with the selection of the archive material, on the design of the
> exhibition, or on contributing to PR (text writing, for example)? Paul could also
> talk to her about the feasibility of the project. The placement will be between
> two and three months long. With this in mind, what is the best moment in the
> preparation phase to 'step in'? It would of course be best if the official opening
> of the exhibition were to fall within the placement period.

Conclusion

Networking is, in short, an important competence on the road to finding a placement. It's something everyone can learn. Some people do it naturally, others need
some incentive and self-imposed discipline. As a student, you are in the ideal position to develop into a good networker. Thanks to all those students and student
associations, you have a massive network. Also, everyone is in the same boat, and
this lowers the thresholds for starting a conversation.

Networking for a placement does not have to be more difficult than networking for
a new bicycle. It is all about having the right *mentality*:

> What it comes down to in practice is reacting to signals of acquaintances: answer-
> ing their questions, sending them things that they might need, sending them a
> token of thanks when they have done you a favour, and so on – in short, treating
> your contacts and the people you meet through them in a social, friendly, and
> sympathetic way. Once you adopt this mentality, you will notice that you will start
> enjoying it, even though the results might not be immediately visible. (Van Eeden,
> 2004: 36)

Before moving on to Step 5, applying for a placement, here is a list of all the dos and
don'ts of networking:

Do's

- Make sure that you are aware of what the people in your network are interested
  in.
- If you hear anything interesting about these topics, pass it on to them.
- When someone from your network asks for help, be prepared to do him/her a
  favour.

- Send your networking partners a token of thanks after you've spoken with them. Do this as quickly as possible and refer to the topics discussed or agreements made to make sure that your networking partners remember the conversation.

Don'ts

- Don't get in touch with someone only when you need their help.
- Don't put people under pressure to help you.
- Don't be impatient: getting a result from networking takes time.
- Trust is an important principle of networking. Don't do anything that could damage people's trust in you.
- Don't make empty promises. If you promise something, live up to it – preferably without waiting too long. That way, you present yourself as a trustworthy person.

Step 5 Applying for a Placement

While busy networking, you may suddenly find yourself in the middle of the application process. This often happens quite unexpectedly. Like a treasure hunter, you suddenly stumble across what you were looking for: a placement that appeals to you. But how will you know? Simple: your heart starts beating faster. It is a bit like seeing a nice car ('I'd like to have one of those') or a nice leather jacket ('If only I had the money . . .'). It is a feeling you might recognize from when you were writing down your aim for your personal profile. The circle should now be complete: the placement you found matches the aim you described in your functional résumé.

There are two types of applications, namely *solicited* applications and *unsolicited* applications. If you come across a placement in an advertisement, you can send a *solicited* application. A proper advertisement gives a detailed job description, and this can help you choose an approach.

If you want to do a placement with a particular organization but don't know if they offer any placement positions, you can send them an *unsolicited* application. Large organizations are used to receiving unsolicited applications for placements and jobs. You won't know the addressee in this case, so you have to learn as much as possible about the company in advance. You could call this a 'cold' unsolicited application. This is often a successful way of applying because it gives the addressee the opportunity to take control. In a way, you anticipate a vacancy, and the addressee can *create* a placement position for you. He or she can see where you might fit in and discuss this with you.

'Warm' unsolicited applications are even more successful. This is where you send an application, without there being a vacancy, to someone from your network. Someone you have met before or whom you know through someone else will be more interested in your letter and will put more effort into helping you. This kind of application is often less formal than cold unsolicited applications.

If you ask students how they found their placement, 40% will say they sent a cold unsolicited application and another 40% will mention warm unsolicited applications (via family, friends, fellow students, and lecturers). Only 20% will tell you that they found their placement by responding to an advertisement (*i.e.* a solicited application).

Technically speaking, solicited applications are broadly the same as unsolicited ones, which is why the substeps 'preparation', 'Curriculum Vitae', 'application letter', and 'interview' apply to both types of applications. If something applies to unsolicited applications only, the text will mention this.

5.1   Preparation

The key to a successful application, in any form, is preparation. When applying for a placement, your degree programme takes up a significant part of the preparation. From this moment on, you will find out how hard it is to 'serve', on the one hand, those involved in your degree programme (after all, you want your placement to be awarded with credits) and, on the other hand, your future placement provider.

First, your degree programme: you listed the placement criteria of your degree programme in the orientation phase. At this stage, it is time to ask your placement coordinator if you really meet the requirements to enter the labour market in search of a placement. Make sure you posed the following questions to the right people, as the responsibility for answering these questions often lies with different people (*e.g.* your supervisor, your placement coordinator, and your lecturer).

- Do you meet the entry requirements? (Have you earned sufficient credits?)
- Does your degree programme approve of your choice of industry, the type of organization, and the kind of assignment?
- Are you sure you are allowed to start your placement during the period you have in mind? Will you be back in time (for your visa or scholarship, for instance)?

Next comes the organization. When preparing for the actual application it is important that you know what your target audience (the recipient of your application letter or e-mail, or the selection committee) pays attention to:

1.   Placement providers will pay attention to your *profile*, the combination of your knowledge, skills, degree programme, and experience. The profile they are looking for is reflected in the job requirements. It is likely you won't meet *all* requirements, but you can present your profile in such a way that it matches the job requirements as closely as possible.
2.   Secondly, carefully consider what your motivations and ambitions are; you will be asked to talk about them. Placement providers also pay attention to your skills and characteristics. Just listing them as you have done in your personal profile won't be enough; you will have to prepare examples for every competence you wish to discuss.
3.   Finally, placement providers focus on your level of working and thinking. Positions in organizations are often classified into three levels: senior second-

ary vocational level, higher professional level, and academic level. If you are applying for a placement on a higher professional level, for example, the selection committee will want to find out whether you can think and work at that level. This does not necessarily mean that you need to have a degree on that level; what matters is that you are able to work independently, that you have the ability to express ideas about the execution of tasks, that you can rapidly gain an overview, and that you possess a wide and thorough knowledge as well as a solid general education (see also: <www.internshipguide.elevenpub.com>).

With this in mind, there are two ways to prepare yourself. Firstly: never respond to an advertisement or tip before you have gathered as much information as possible about the position, the department, the organization, the culture, and corporate culture of the country in question. You can find this information on websites, in annual reports (social and otherwise), in corporate newsletters, in articles about the company, in any relevant literature, and . . . via your network (Step 4!)

Secondly: stick to the organization's application procedure. There's a good chance the website gives you an idea of how the company prefers to be approached. This is a very useful tip for any application and the only preparation that truly matters. Some employers do not appreciate it if you call them; they prefer to work via social media, their website, or e-mail. If calling is an option, do not call them out of the blue, but prepare thoroughly. You are going to leave a first impression and you can only leave it once:

- Write down the questions you want to ask as well as the answers that are given. You can then quote from these answers in your letter. That way, the addressee sees that you are a good listener and feels personally addressed and taken seriously. The letter will give them the feeling that they already know you a bit.
- Do not only prepare what you want to ask, but also what you want to *say*. Show the addressee that you have done some research; mention the latest news or a project of the organization, and show them how motivated you are. Tell them you are interested and, if possible, show them your respect for their culture.
- Make sure that your cover letter and CV are as good as ready, and send them to your contact person within three days after the conversation. Announce this during the conversation: ask the addressee if they want to receive the letter by e-mail or by regular mail. Also, make sure you have spelled their name and job title correctly.

This way, you can demonstrate various competences in a single conversation: accuracy, decisiveness, motivation, empathy, intercultural competences, and reliability.

5.2 Curriculum Vitae

Your CV is a summary of the education and experiences you have had in your life until now, and is generally no longer than one to one-and-a-half A4-sized pages. One page is probably enough for newcomers on the labour market.

Your CV is the key document in the application process. It accompanies your application letter or letter of motivation. Even though it is an attachment, your CV is your primary sales pitch. You can see it as a business card, but even more as a sales document. In fact, you could consider it a brochure that you use to present yourself. Your aim is to motivate the reader to invite you for an interview. This is important; the purpose of a CV is not, as is often thought, to make sure you get the placement. You use your CV to recommend yourself as a suitable candidate for an interview. The aim of the *interview* is then to get you that placement or job.

Your CV, in short, is burdened with some difficult tasks. Personnel officers (human resource staff) and managers have the thankless task of selecting the right candidate out of often big piles of letters. You do not want your letter to end up on a pile marked 'Doubtful' or 'Rejected', but on the 'Invite for an Interview' pile.

1. Your CV's first task, therefore, is to attract attention. Do not take that too literally, though. Using coloured paper and a showy typeface or stating unusual hobbies is often counterproductive.

2. Your CV's second task is to enable the reader to judge whether you qualify for the position. This means that the reader should be able to see at a glance what your knowledge and experience is.

3. Your CV's third task is to show the reader that you are serious. By demonstrating neatness, formulating sentences correctly, and avoiding mistakes, you show

the reader that you possess a number of basic competences that are expected of every employee. You are expected to take the organization seriously, to approach the selection committee with respect, and to be accurate and precise. In other words: you use your CV to show that you can score when it matters.

This is not as hard as you think. To compile your CV, you just need to return to your personal profile and summarize the section of your profile that describes what you know and what your abilities are. The section that expresses what you *want* is reserved for your application letter.

Start compiling your CV as quickly as possible and update it from time to time. This will save you the trouble of trying to remember your graduation date every time you see an interesting placement opportunity, and you'll avoid forgetting to mention some summer course you once took.

5.2.1   Basic CV

No two applications are alike, simply because no two placements are alike. Every application letter you send focuses on the *characteristics of the position you are applying for*. Your CV, enclosed with your letter, will also differ a bit with each application; you highlight the experience and competences that match the characteristics of the position you are applying for. It would be nice if you can show the addressee that your CV is directed specifically at him or her. You can do this by simply putting the dates of your letter and the advertisement at the top of your CV, or by emphasizing specific items in your CV. The best way to make such a customized CV is to use a *basic CV* that you adapt to the positions you're applying for.

Your basic CV lists *all* training, jobs, courses, and other experiences you have had in your life. It is far too elaborate to be used for actually applying, though; your basic CV is therefore *not* meant for potential employers. You write it for yourself, to get an overview of your experiences, including dates (in years). When preparing your CV for a solicited application, you select the study programmes and experience relevant to that placement or job and leave out the rest. Keep in mind that there is no single right way to create a CV. The purpose is to create interest in you as a potential intern or employee . . . Please try to find examples to decide how you can effectively organize your education, experience, other qualifications and skills so the most information can be found in fifteen seconds.

Apart from getting a complete overview of your experiences, there's another reason why you should draw up a basic CV. CVs need to be neat, flawless, and clearly formulated, so writing one takes a lot of time. That's why many people are not particularly fond of this task. When you invest time in writing a basic CV, you will save time on all your future applications; you can easily adapt your basic CV to the positions you are applying for without having to write an entire CV over and over again.

To make it easier for you, there are examples galore from which to choose a template. A CV consists of the following items:

CURRICULUM VITAE

Personal details

Name	First names, Surname and possibly Title and Calling name
Address	Street name, House number
Postcode	Zip code
City	Place of residence
Date of birth	Date of birth
Place of Birth	Place of birth
Gender	Male/Female
LinkedIn Profile	Web address LinkedIn
Telephone number	Fixed and Mobile telephone number
E-mail	E-mail address

Education(ranging from most recent to earliest)

Year (xxxx-xxxx)	Course/Qualification/Programme: University, City, Country, Degree, Subjects, Major
	Type of certificate, (expected) year of graduation, field of study, final-year project or thesis with possible specialization, placements, courses (optional or compulsory) relevant to the placement or job position
	Preparatory secondary vocational education/senior general secondary education/pre-university education: type of certificate, year of graduation, examination subjects

Work experience (ranging from most recent to earliest)

Year (xxxx-xxxx)	Name of company/institution, City, Country, your position/title, your responsibilities/description of tasks

Additional activities

Year (incl. duration)	Relevant placements, initiatives, volunteer work or sports activities that could be relevant to the employer; all activities that demonstrate leadership skills, organizational skills, or perseverance are worth mentioning (state the company, your position, the dates, and the tasks)

Additional information

Language skills	Languages, preferably with the official codes of fluency (see CEFR in Section 5.6.1 and the Europass CV on <www.internshipguide.elevenpub.com> for more information)
Driving licence	Type of driving licence, Year of driving test
Computer skills	Computer software that you have a thorough command of
Leisure activities	Interests and hobbies (not too many)
Publications	Title, Medium, Publisher, Place, Year, Page number

When explicitly requested:

Photo	A clear, suitable photo of yourself
References	Name, Employer, Contact

You could also mention the items 'Objective' (see 'Profile'), a 'Summary of Skills and Qualifications,' and 'Research and Project Experience'. Once your basic CV is finished, ask someone from a different discipline from yours to take a look at it. First ask them to comment on the content. Ask them what job they think your CV is suitable for, and whether it makes clear which tasks you are interested in and what your competences are.

You may encounter the following problems while writing your basic CV:

- *A gap in your CV.* If you have taken some time off during your studies, for instance, employers will consider this a 'gap' in your CV and will probably jump to conclusions. The best thing to do is to account for these empty spaces by mentioning useful activities you were involved in during that period; if you have travelled, for example, put this in your basic CV. If you have never been abroad but have done a lot of babysitting or helped organize an event, write this down in *marketable terms* (focused on employers). Think carefully about all the activities you were involved in during that period and write them down in your basic CV. You can then try to group together all these activities under one heading. It's great to be able to say, for example, that you gained a lot of experience in various jobs during that period in order to get a better idea of potential degree programmes.
- *Diploma.* Employers like to see that you have completed your training with a degree or certificate. It shows them that you finish what you started and what your level of knowledge is. It is therefore important to state your graduation date for every study programme you completed. A study programme that you *didn't* complete is, for that reason, a problem for your CV. If that is the case, explain in a few sentences how this could have happened. It sounds better to

say that you were made a job offer that you simply couldn't refuse than to say that the course was too tough for you. You can add this explanation to your basic CV.

- *Experience.* If you gained experience in an entirely different field from the position you are applying for, you will have to explain why you are changing course and why you think you are up to it. This might present a problem if your CV doesn't provide clues to verify this. It can give employers the idea that you are unpredictable (*i.e.* you might want to leave again the moment you are hired) or reckless, or that you do not take the placement seriously. In this case, you should write a well-phrased and well-founded explanation as to why you want to change your field of work; you can add this to your basic CV too.

Once you have written down all your training and experience in a basic CV, you should update it regularly. Note down every article you publish, every workshop you earn a diploma for, and every job you hold; then, when applying for a job or placement, the only thing left to do is to delete irrelevant information from your CV, leaving only information that is relevant. This way, all your CVs will correspond to reality, but practically none of them will be exactly the same. Do make sure that your CV contains the same information when you post it in different places (*e.g.* LinkedIn).

5.2.2   Customized (Chronological) CV

You will only have to start thinking about the reader once you start drawing up a customized, chronological CV. He or she should be easily able to form an impression of you – preferably at a single glance. The layout of your CV can help you direct the reader's attention, thus increasing the chance that the impression you want to convey will come across. Try to imagine what they would be interested in and ask yourself which competences might be relevant to the offered position. Also keep in mind that the reader will compare your CV with others. Pay attention to your English. If you choose to use British English or American English, be consistent. The following section will discuss the content-related requirements of a customized CV as well as the requirements regarding layout, style, and accuracy.

The most important element of your CV is, of course, the content. Every word you use may have a positive or negative effect on the impression you make on the reader. These are things that you often overlook, which is why it is so important to have someone else read your CV before sending it off.

Ideally, a CV is:

1. Complete

   It provides a complete overview of all your achievements: mention everything that is relevant, even if it is not directly related to the placement position. Travelling, social positions, and hobbies often tell a great deal about your personality and they point to competences that the selection committee may consider useful for the placement. If any particular achievement was the result of teamwork, mention exactly what you contributed.

2. Concise

   The text should be concise but coherent. Use only abbreviations after having introduced the full term first.

3. Orderly

   Differentiate between main aspects and related aspects. Describe in more detail experiences that you would like to stand out; experiences with longer descriptions automatically look more important. If you wish to show a particular background development, make sure it stands out clearly. For one, be consistent in describing your experiences – by letting the word 'marketing' return in several subsequent experiences, for example.

4. Clear

   Make sure the text makes for pleasant reading. Avoid the use of jargon, unless you are certain that by using terminology you make a good impression on the selection committee. But, even in that case, try not to overdo it.

5. Interesting

   Try to keep the reader's attention. Do not just write down that you worked at some place, because that doesn't provide enough information. Describe what the job involved: in marketable terms, what were your tasks and responsibilities?

6. Professional

   Be neither modest nor boastful. Stay professional, even if contact with the addressee has been relatively informal. Do not add courses that you have not really done, even though *you were planning to do them.* They often stick out when the jobs you describe are of a lower level than what you would have been capable of after completing such an imaginary course. If you have been invited for an interview and they ask you questions about that course that you have trouble answering, you can say goodbye to that placement.

7. Concrete

   Try to illustrate your activities with numbers where possible: were you in charge of 8 or 120 people? Did you have a €2,000 or €20,000 budget? Did you organize an event for 25 or 2,500 people? Did the website you built get 1,000 or 100,000 unique visitors daily?

8. Appropriate

This is a customized CV. This means not only that you leave out any irrelevant achievements and experiences from your basic CV, but also that you adapt the *style* of your CV to the placement you are applying for. If you are applying for an editorial placement, do not just *mention* that you have writing experience but *show* it.

You must have noticed that, in describing the *content* of a customized CV, mentioning the form is inevitable. The format requirements simply determine the text type. You could, however, also add something important to a customized CV that would change it considerably from the previously discussed basic CV. In *two cases* it is possible to supplement the components discussed in the previous section with a profile or a summary. When you prepare a CV for a networking conversation, it is recommended you add a *profile*, which you place below your personal details:

Profile

For example: 'Multilingual business student with international financial experience and ability to develop business relationships seeking a financial consulting career in life insurance and pensions.'

If you prepare a CV without a cover letter it is recommended you include a *summary*. When applying for placements, you will frequently be asked to mail your CV without a cover letter. If so, you can add a short motivation to the e-mail body – but as they often only print the CV and not the e-mail, the addressee will only get to see your printed CV. In that case, you can add the heading 'Summary', followed by a summary of your application, to the bottom of your CV:

Summary

For example: 'I am currently (September 2011) writing my thesis for the Master's degree programme in International Business (IB). I am also in the selection process for the Master's degree programme in Journalism at the same university. I have an affinity with various media (new and old), partly because of my minors in Communication Sciences. With a bit of help I think I could gain a thorough understanding of the software mentioned in your advertisement. English poses no problem for me; a Master's degree certificate in IB automatically includes the title "near-native speaker". In addition, I have lived in America for eighteen months in total.

I will be on holiday from 5 July until the beginning of August. After that, I will be available for a placement with your department for four days a week or, if possible, half a day more.'

A CV needs to provide a quick and clear overview, which is why there is a fixed number of requirements regarding layout:

1. A customized CV is no longer than one-and-a-half pages of A4. Better yet is to limit yourself to only one page of A4.

2. A CV is a CV only if it says so *at the top*, so do not forget to add this. Also mention at the top what the CV is an attachment to, for example: 'Attachment to cover letter Philips, 12 October 2012' or 'Re: position of training advisor at JVC Productions'.

3. There is some debate as to whether to mention your latest training first or to draw up your CV in a logical chronological order. The reader will be primarily interested in your most recent experience, so it is recommended you mention your most recent training and experience first. This is currently also the most common practice. You put the years on the left side and a description of the job or training one tab to the right. Avoid the use of months unless something took up only a short period of time.

4. Try to get rid of the CV problems discussed in the previous section. Fill the 'gaps' in your CV with experiences gained during those periods, explain why you did not finish a course, and add, as a reason for a clear switch in your interests, that you were in need of a fresh challenge. Be prepared to answer questions about this during an interview.

5. A CV must be free of mistakes and completely truthful. Employers can easily verify exaggerations and made-up additions. They will google your name to see what kind of person you are. Try to come across as a serious person; use a *serious* e-mail address, for instance. If your e-mail address is 'stunningly_gorgeous_anna@hotmail.com', it will raise a few eyebrows at the least and, in the worst case, will give people a reason not to invite you for an interview. Also make sure that you can be reached at the provided addresses. Do not turn off your phone during the application procedure and check your e-mail daily.

6. While a CV is a *list* of experiences, there should also be something to *read*. You can reserve some space in the right-hand column to describe in prose the courses you followed, the essays you've written, and the jobs you've had. Put yourself in the reader's shoes when doing this.

7. A well-written CV is characterized by elements that are different from usual. It's possible that you have remarkable skills or experience, or that your professional experience demonstrates that you have looked at a professional field from a great many angles. You may also have taught courses from which one

can conclude that you are an expert in a particular field. You can show such skills or experience by describing your former jobs using the same terminology or by subtly indicating that there is a clear upward trend in the level at which you work (Bolte, 2003).

Here are some basic tips from Bolte (2003: 70) regarding the style and form of a CV:

Sentence structure
- Use short, simple sentences. Write, for example: 'Chaired the newsletter's editorial board' instead of 'Chaired the editorial meetings of the biweekly company magazine'.
- Write as 'actively' as possible. In other words, write in the simple past as much as possible, and avoid the passive voice and the present perfect and past perfect tenses. Write, for example, 'I organized a conference', rather than 'Responsible for organizing a conference' or 'I have organized' or 'I had organized a conference'.
- Do try to avoid excessive use of the words 'I' and 'my', though; it may give the impression that you focus more on yourself than on the placement provider.

Vocabulary
- Be as transparent as possible. 'Assistance service points' could be a well-known term for you and your former colleagues, but the reader may not know what it means.
- Be concrete. Saying that you sat on the board of student society 'Be2' from 2008 until 2009 is not enough. What did you actually accomplish during that period? In addition, your work experience as a call centre employee is of interest because it shows that you worked regular hours. But did you achieve the maximum bonus because you performed well above your target? Or were you voted one of the fifty best employees and did you get a voucher for this? Write it all down. Make your achievements known.
- Use everyday words. Avoid unnecessary jargon; don't expect the reader to know the abbreviations you know. For example, it may be more than clear to you that your specialization 'CE' stands for 'Commercial Economy', but some readers won't have any idea what it means.

Form/layout
- Limit yourself to two separate sheets of white A4 paper.

- Maintain a calm layout, using wide, white margins on all sides (2.5 cm) and a familiar font, such as Verdana or Georgia. Align the text to the left.
- Use subheadings, but do not vary the text size. Do not underline anything and use only boldface for headings.
- Do not add images. Only add your photo to your CV if you have been explicitly asked to do so or if it is customary in the country of the placement-providing organization.

If you meet all these requirements, you can be sure that you have a good CV. If your CV is the reason you are not invited for an interview, you can be fairly certain that the placement provider has rightly concluded that you are not the right person for the placement or that there are just too many qualified candidates. After all, the more candidates there are, the stricter the selection procedure.

Maryse has made various attempts to obtain a placement with a commercial broadcaster. She's a Journalism student and is interested in *infotainment*, so she's applying to the editorial teams of three commercial news programmes. To her surprise, none of the editors she has written to has bothered to invite her for an interview. Maryse asks her supervising lecturer for advice. How is it possible that she doesn't seem to qualify for placements that students before her did get accepted for? The lecturer seems to know why. Maryse very truthfully put 'Pierrefonds' as her place of residence on her CV. The lecturer suggests that it may be wiser in this case to replace it with the address of a friend in Paris. Broadcast editors, especially commercial ones, often assume that more rural areas are not only terribly far away, but also that students from those 'faraway places' are unwilling to move temporarily to Paris for their placement – while, to those students, it is the most natural thing in the world. After Maryse has replaced the old address on her CV with a temporary address in Paris, she is indeed accepted.

Maryse wasn't really lying. Once accepted for the placement, she's going to have to move to Paris anyway. Still, there are plenty of people who tell blatant lies in their CV in order to qualify for an interview. It is foolish to make up things about your training or exaggerate about past jobs. Not only because – once you start your placement – it will soon come to light that you don't possess the made-up experience or skill (and you will be prematurely dismissed), but also because employers make use of *pre-employment screenings*. They hire specialized research agencies to verify the information that applicants put in their CV. Some employers require a certificate of good conduct, which may be obtained from the local authorities. The certificate, required when applying for jobs such as that of a teacher or taxi driver, shows that you have no criminal record.

Whether it is advisable to include a photo in your CV differs from country to country. This is common practice in Germany, where you can even have professional photos taken for each specific application (Boland, 2010: 68). Then again, applicants in Germany are also required to present a comprehensive *Bewerbungsmappe*. In the United States, however, a picture in your CV is out of the question because of fear of discrimination.

5.2.3   Skills CV

A chronological CV is regarded by some employers as an old-fashioned, somewhat dull list of facts. While it does give an idea of what the CV's owner has done over the years, it says little about the actual *person*. For that reason, more and more placement providers want to see a so-called 'skills CV'. In a skills CV, you demonstrate the expertise and skills you have acquired throughout your life by describing your experiences.

A skills CV divides your experiences into achievements, competences and skills, roles, and professional experience. The arrangement is thematic, not chronological. Other names for a skills CV are therefore 'thematic CV' or 'functional CV'. The skills CV differs from the chronological CV not only in arrangement but also in style: a skills CV contains more running sentences (prose); you use it to *describe* yourself fully.

The different components of a skills CV are:
- the aforementioned 'profile' (if requested);
- your personal details;
- the position you are applying for, or, in the case of an unsolicited application, a description of the work you would like to do;
- your competences and skills, including language and computer skills; if you have many language and computer skills, put them under different headings;
- achievements, such as publications, projects, or the organization of events;
- education, possibly including exam subjects, specializations, and the topic of your bachelor's or master's thesis; for convenience, it is best to put this section in chronological order;
- professional experience, focusing on those experiences and roles that fit the position you are applying for; choose between a summary of your experience written in prose and a chronological listing of former jobs;
- interests and additional information.

Like the chronological CV, you can also base your skills CV on your basic CV. It is a bit more challenging than making a chronological CV, however, because you have to try to give descriptions that are positive yet fairly neutral at the same time. When describing your competences and achievements, there is a set of rules you can use. The most important rule is that you take only those things from your basic CV that are relevant to the position you are applying for. It is also helpful to use the STAR method (see Section 6.1.3) to give concrete examples of your abilities.

The Position or Desired Work Tasks

If a skills CV is requested in a placement advertisement, it is sufficient to just mention that particular vacancy. This type of CV is more often required for unsolicited applications, however. The addressee won't know what to expect from someone following your degree programme, and will therefore hope to get a clearer picture of you by reading about your skills. If there is no ready-made placement within the organization, the addressee will also want to know what kind of placement assignment you would like to do and what your degree programme allows you to do. You could mention a number of potential assignments under the heading 'desired work tasks'. Emphasize that it is 'either . . . or' and that you cannot fit all assignments into one placement. Keep the length of the placement in mind and discuss the feasibility of a potential assignment with your lecturer. After all, you can do more in a nine-month placement than in a placement of only three months.

95

Skills CV: Overview of Your Competences and Skills
1. *What* you have learned is important, not *where* you learned it. Do not limit yourself to the competences you have acquired in your work, but also mention the competences you acquired in courses and in your spare time.
2. Supplement competences and skills with *facts*. Do not just mention the name of the software you are familiar with, but also what it can do. Describe your command of a foreign language using the Common European Framework of Reference (CEFR): a framework, put together by the Council of Europe, which classifies language proficiency levels. It means more to a practised reader that you have a level C1 command of Spanish according to the CEFR than if you were simply to say that you 'have a command of both written and spoken Spanish', especially because the CEFR is more reliable. After all, you are allowed to state

your language proficiency only in terms of the CEFR if it is the result of an officially recognized test. Europass has an online wizard that enables you to easily create a list of your language skills.

3. Avoid contradictions; *make choices*. If you say that you 'are very precise' and 'always see the greater picture', then this says nothing about you: it is a contradiction. People who are very precise are often not as successful in forming an overview. Neither is it a good idea to say that you are a 'team player' but can 'work well independently' at the same time. What would you like to do the most? What are you really like?

4. Try to be as *clear* as possible. You can do this by using examples. If you say that you are perseverant, you are making a rather general statement; if you add that despite suffering from glandular fever you still managed to complete enough courses in your first year at university in order to be able to continue into your second year, you provide evidence for this quality. A great tool for this is the STAR method, which will be discussed in Step 6 (The Interview).

Achievements

1. Achievements differ considerably from competences and skills because they can be made visible and verifiable. Use a separate paragraph to describe them. Achievements include matters such as articles published under your name, prizes you have won, exhibitions you have organized, items on the radio you were involved in, grants that were awarded to you, etc. Have you published a lot? Then it is best to make a selection under the heading 'publications'. Dissertations and papers can be placed under the heading 'education'.

2. Mention achievements that match the job requirements for the placement. If the placement provider is looking for a person with initiative and you set up a working group once, then mention that here.

3. Don't forget the things you achieved in your spare time.

Professional Experience

It is better to describe your professional experience in terms of the *roles* you fulfilled rather than mentioning the job titles. For example, if you have worked as a team leader for the customer service team of an energy company, describe your role as project leader, instructor, and trainer. Discuss these roles one by one and make clear what you did, what initiatives you took, and what the results were. American companies, in particular, like to know which *targets* you have met.

Consider carefully whether you want to send your skills CV to a placement provider. It is best to save this type of CV for when you are specifically asked to do so. It is always okay to send a customized CV and then highlight your skills in the application letter.

5.3   Application Letter

In an application letter, you make a link between your strengths and the placement. Your core message spells out why you are a suitable candidate. The whole purpose of the letter is not to get accepted immediately, but to be invited for an *interview*, in person or over the phone. You therefore have to present yourself in such a way that the reader will want to meet you.

An application letter is one of the most difficult things to write:
- It is difficult to put your motivation and aim into words.
- It is difficult to describe yourself.
- It is difficult to do this in a clear and concise manner.
- It is difficult to find the balance between *boasting* and *modesty*.
- It is most difficult, however, to have to 'sell' yourself through such a letter.

Many people feel uncomfortable about having to recommend themselves. Still, when it comes to writing application letters, you will often be referred to the AIDA method, which is used for writing sales letters.

> AIDA stands for Attention, Interest, Desire, Action – four terms that are used in marketing. In your application letter you have to try to catch the reader's *attention*; you have to make your letter *stand out* among the other letters. Once you have caught the reader's attention, you have to arouse their *interest* by using the first paragraph to tell the reader that you have the requested profile. This paragraph should therefore not only say, 'I would like to apply for' but should also refer to your CV's personal profile summary you prepared specifically for this placement vacancy. This way, the reader won't put your letter aside but will continue reading. If you see yourself as a product that needs to be sold, the second part of your letter should be written in such a way that the reader feels the *desire* to meet you. You can do this by devoting several paragraphs to summarizing your personal selling points: your knowledge and competences. Finally, the last paragraph has the difficult task of motivating the reader to take *action*. It has to express the right mix of modesty and drive. For instance: 'I truly believe that I am the right person for this job.'

Because writing an application letter is such a challenging task, of all types of documents it is the one that is plagiarized the most. Many people argue that when writing their application letter it is better to steal something good than to make something bad. They have a point. Not everyone is good at writing letters. That is why there are companies who gladly take care of this bothersome task for you. You can have your application letter written by someone else for €35, and for an additional €15 they will also draw up your CV. But that does not make it very personal. It is perfectly all right, however, to copy the paragraph structure of a letter from someone whose letters prove to be successful.

Perhaps you think the AIDA method is a bit over the top. However, the purpose of the method is not to turn your letter into a rambling sales pitch, but to teach you that you are writing your letter *for someone else*. This is called *target-oriented* writing, which requires you to delve deeply into the reader's mind.

5.3.1   Application Letter for an Advertised Position

Applying for a placement vacancy has real use only if the advertisement triggers something inside of you.

If you approach placement advertisements in a more rational manner, you may be tempted to respond to many advertised vacancies at once. You may qualify for more than one vacancy, for example, because your degree programme is in demand or because your management experience makes you unique. Some students send off dozens of letters at the same time, with the motto 'more is better'. This is a bad idea, not only because it is impossible to write a position-oriented application letter this way, but also because using this type of overproduction will lead to mistakes.

> Alicia Smith, lecturer at a university of applied sciences, asks the careers advisor of the same university to have a talk with one of her Indonesian students. The student, Phone Me Janita Lahuyantha, wrote her an e-mail in poor English asking for help in finding a placement. She is looking for a placement that matches her specialization in the field of 'Children's Rights Advocacy' as part of her degree programme in Development Aid. She has sent more than seventy letters to organizations all over the world, and sends letters daily to a company that addresses this issue. The location of the placement is of no importance to her: she applies just as easily to companies in Kabul and Leeds as to companies in Singapore and Moscow. Time is running out; according to her degree programme, the placement should start within four months. She has received no positive replies yet to any of her letters. There was one UN department in Indonesia that initially showed interest, but they cancelled her placement because she was 'overqualified'. The careers advisor invites Phone Me to her office. Before the interview, she asked Alicia about the origins of

'Phone Me', an unusual name. Alicia told her that Phone Me was born shortly after her parents got a telephone. She also has friends who are called 'VCR' or 'Video'; names given by parents who were so very proud of their newly ac-quired device that they named their child after it. The careers advisor has also closely studied Phone Me's CV, which contains an enormous, impressive list of experiences and training. At the top of page 1 is a photograph of Phone Me, dressed in her Indonesian school uniform – white blouse and black tie – looking sternly into the camera. The photo is outdated; Phone Me's hair is short now, and she wears glasses. In her office, the careers advisor asks Phone Me why she uses an old photograph. Phone Me says it's her official photo and that it is the only one she has. 'Can't you ask a fellow student to take a more cur-rent photo?' asks the careers advisor. Phone Me replies that she will certainly try to do that. The careers advisor then moves to the subject of Phone Me's CV and application letter. Phone Me uses her e-mail address, Janita.Lahuyantha@email.com for correspondence. Has she taken into account that 'Phone Me' may be regarded as a somewhat odd name in the Western world? An Asian girl with a name like that does have certain connotations . . . Phone Me says that she cannot change the name in her CV because the references she mentions only know her by that name; if a placement provider were to inquire about 'Janita', the referent would probably not know her . . . The careers advisor advises her to at least use the name Janita in her letter and e-mail, and to put 'Phone Me' between brackets in the personal details of her CV. For Phone Me it's a painful, yet probably also useful, piece of advice . . . Within three weeks, Janita, under the name Janita and without the photo in her CV, has found a placement with a children's aid organization in Pakistan.

If you are capable of communicating openly, if you stick to agreements, and if you can make choices quickly, you may want to apply for more than one placement at a time. However, be prepared to make some difficult decisions: you may be offered the placement of your second choice while awaiting the results of the application for your dream placement. In the case of UNICEF, for example, the standard length of the application procedure is four months. What should you do? Do you have time to wait for your dream placement or should you seize the first opportunity and accept a slightly less attractive placement? This is where preconditions will play a decisive role.

A well-written solicited application letter consists of the following parts:
1. the recipient's full address: name of organization, name of addressee, address;
2. a subject: 'Application for vacancy number 10.112' or 'Placement in the Eco-nomics Department';
3. a personal salutation: 'Dear Ms Smith';
4. information about where you found the placement advertisement, in one paragraph using only one sentence;

5. the reason you are applying for this vacancy (*i.e.* your motivation), in one paragraph;
6. the reason why you – given your experience, particular competences, training – qualify for the placement, in one or two paragraphs;
7. a final paragraph stating, in one or two sentences, that you are willing to discuss your application in an interview;
8. a valediction (or 'complimentary close' in American) and signature: 'Sincerely', your signature, name, and address;
9. a reference to your attached CV, in one sentence at the bottom of the page.

Mention the name and location of the placement advertisement at the top of the CV and make sure that the letter and the CV have a corresponding layout. When sending them as e-mail attachments, it is especially important that the addressee can clearly identify both documents at the printer (as those company printers are often shared by different people).

Making sure that the letter has a proper structure is just the beginning. How can you make your sentences run smoothly, and, more importantly, how can you get your motivation across to the reader? There are plenty of sample letters that you can use, as well as keywords that your addressee mentioned in the phone call, but how do you make your letter appealing? The most important guideline is to always try to sound *authentic*, to make the letter really show who you are. This requires a certain degree of frankness that you can teach yourself by practising, and there are numerous books, not to mention your careers advisor and your lecturer, who can help you in this.

In addition, just as for your CV, the overall look of your application letters is very important. They serve as a business card and give a first (or second) impression that is crucial to the decision whether or not to invite you to attend an interview. Your letter and CV go hand in hand.

5.3.2   Unsolicited Application Letter

The layout of an unsolicited application letter does not differ all that much from the layout of a solicited application letter; they are, however, discussed separately. The most important difference in layout is that Parts 2 and 4 of the structure discussed in the previous section are left out. Then there are some content-related differences: firstly, your *approach* in an unsolicited application is different. You will usually know a lot less about the department and the organization than if you were to re-spond to a placement advertisement. Unsolicited applications therefore require you to put more effort into research prior to applying. You have to call the department or organization to ask them if it is possible to send an unsolicited application and, if it is, whom to address it to. You cannot ask just any staff member because many of them will say 'no,' while the manager might be desperate for students on place-ment. This means that you also have to look for the *right* informant. This requires networking, something you probably already did in Step 4.

The most important content-related difference between an unsolicited and a so-licited application has to do with the presence or absence of a set of tasks. The or-ganization that you write an unsolicited application to has not yet thought about a possible placement *assignment*. As no thought has yet gone into the appointment of a student on placement, no thought has gone into a possible *set of tasks* either. This also means that the organization has not yet considered the required *profile*; there's a great chance that they will ask you, 'What can you do for us?' You might think it is a topsy-turvy situation. Once the manager or project leader has indicated that he could benefit from appointing you – after your phone call he realized that there is plenty of work for you within the department or project – he puts the ball in your court. It is up to you to formulate a potential assignment. This might be an uncomfortable situation for you if you have never been on placement before. After all, you don't know what exactly a placement involves, nor what kind of assignment would meet your degree programme's criteria. Besides, you also have to be able to assess the level and potential length of the placement.

You should therefore get an idea of placement assignments you are allowed to do as part of your programme before you submit any unsolicited applications. Try to make a list of potential placement assignments. You can use networking for this: ask fellow students what tasks they had to perform on placement. You can also ask your lecturer to go through various scenarios with you. In addition, you can consult placement reports of fellow students; these are often made public. Most importantly, you have to ask yourself what the organization you are applying to *needs*.

When exploring, try to get a clear idea of the length of a placement. Some assignments can be rounded off successfully within two months, while others need four. Also, ask your lecturer for the required *output*; will you be asked to draw up a placement report only, or do you have to add a research report or consultation paper?

An unsolicited application letter pays more attention to your general profile than a solicited application does, and contains the following:

1. the recipient's full address: name of organization, name of addressee, address;
2. a subject: *e.g.* 'unsolicited application for a placement within the Economics Department';
3. a personal salutation: 'Dear Mr Johnson';
4. the reason you are applying to this particular department and this particular organization (in other words, your motivation), in one paragraph;
5. the contribution that you – given your experience, particular competences, training – can make as a student on placement, in one or two paragraphs;
6. a final paragraph stating that you are willing to discuss your application in an interview, in one paragraph of one or two sentences;
7. a valediction and signature: 'Sincerely', your signature, name, and address;
8. a reference to the attached CV, in one sentence at the bottom of the page.

When there's no placement advertisement to respond to, you have to make an extra effort to win the reader over. More importantly, you have to tailor the letter specifically to him or her. You can do this by looking for keywords that the organization uses in the field you are interested in. Social media such as Twitter and LinkedIn can help you with this. Talking to employees is another means of finding out what jargon and current terminology is used by the organization.

By mentioning these terms in your letter, you show them not only that you have studied the company, but also that you understand what they are doing. If you have an idea of the tone of voice used in the organization, it is easier to prepare for a potential interview.

5.4   Digital Application

Sometimes it's not possible to contact the placement-providing organization directly. Large organizations such as the UN or departments of the European Commission do not accept normal application letters for placements. Placements with these institutions are in such high demand that they have decided to work with digital application forms. Most of them provide an application protocol on their website, a procedure that may take several months. Part of the protocol involves application forms that you have to fill in digitally. Unfortunately, this is the only way; in most cases, there is no shorter or more direct route. Only if you know a staff member of one of the offices or branches personally, is there a slim chance you may circumvent the application protocol, get the opportunity to lobby, and sometimes receive a quicker response.

In principle, it shouldn't matter to the placement provider *how* you send your application letter; by regular mail or by digital mail. However, a study by Dutch career platform Intermediair shows that employers judge digital applications to be of lower quality than applications posted in the regular way. The 150 human resource managers who participated in this study gave the average posted application letter a 7 and the average digital one a 6.3. CVs received higher marks, but those posted by regular mail were also graded higher than those posted by e-mail: 7.2 for the paper CV versus 6.3 for the digital option (Boland 2010: 70).

If the organization asks you to apply via e-mail, find out what exactly is expected of you. Many placement providers will ask for an e-mail with your CV only. You can often e-mail your CV as a Word or PDF attachment. Do add a short motivation to the body of your mail explaining why you are applying to that organization, and mention the placement vacancy, or – in the case of an unsolicited application – explain what kind of placement you are looking for. This text is a slightly less formal, shorter version of what your application letter would be. Do not let the more informal way of applying mislead you; applying for a placement is always a matter of business. Even when you receive a rather informal e-mail, your reply should still be polite. In many cases, employers are putting you to the test. Your e-mail correspondence may be part of that test. If you are not sure whether the recipient will print the text in your e-mail and you do not want them to base their selection on your CV alone, you might consider adding the heading 'Summary' to your application. Under this heading, you write a brief, business-like summary of the motivation you also put in the e-mail (see also: Section 5.2).

If you are afraid that the recipient might be unable to open the file, it is best to copy and paste the CV into the body of your e-mail. This saves the reader the trouble of having to convert the file to a different version of Word or, in the case of a PDF file, Adobe. It also prevents the attachment from getting lost at a printer. You'll just have to take for granted that you have to simplify the layout of your CV because it may get scrambled in the e-mail programme.

5.5   Applying for a Vacancy via an Employment Agency

There are many employment agencies to be found on the Internet as well as in 'real life'. Their advertisements do not always mention the placement provider's name. In many cases, the companies pay the agency fees, but sometimes the applicants are charged as well. Be sure to keep an eye on the service you get for the money you pay. Apart from the placement provider's address you may also get things in kind. For instance, in exchange for a fee, it is common for employment agencies to arrange your housing and sometimes your visa as well if you are undertaking a placement abroad. Do check whether this fee only includes the agency costs for housing or if it also includes rent. A daily meal is sometimes included as well. Ask your university's placement office if it is an employment agency they know and if they have had good experiences with them.

Applying to organizations is not easy if you don't know anything about them. You have no information about the company's mission, its corporate culture, or projects you could focus on. Fortunately, everyone applying for such a vacancy knows as little as you do, and the placement provider takes this into consideration. You should therefore focus primarily on your ambitions and competences.

5.6   Applying Abroad

There are some universities and universities of applied sciences where 40% of all students do a work placement abroad. Sometimes students are sent abroad by a company – the Ministry of Foreign Affairs, for instance, may send students to embassies and consulates – but students mostly start looking for a placement abroad themselves, which is the case with students of degree programmes in such fields as hotel management and tourism.

You will find that the application procedures in other countries are often very different from what you are used to at home. The methods differ from country to country, but in almost every case your first step in the preparation process is to learn the country's language. After all, in most countries the entire application procedure is conducted in the country's language. Application procedures for international placements or placements with international companies are often in English. It is useful to have a glossary with translations of terms.

Every country has its own 'application culture'. The Dutch organization Expertise in Labour Mobility specializes in providing information about these application cultures. They publish an annual series of manuals called 'Looking for work in . . .' followed by the name of the country in question. You can also try to find an expert (*e.g.* lecturers giving courses in that particular language) or a native of that country. Use the method of networking discussed in Step 4 to ask them for advice.

The language and culture of your host country is discussed below. Topics such as grants, housing, visas, insurance, safety, medical matters, and taxes are discussed in Step 7.

5.6.1   *The Language*

Before you apply for a placement abroad, you should be absolutely certain that you speak the language well enough to get by. If you don't speak the language well enough, your placement is likely to fail. In that case it's better to do a placement in your own country.

> Ingrid, a student of Dutch Literature, wants to do a placement in the United States. She visited two of her friends there during their placement and absolutely loves the country. Her study advisor told her that placements abroad are also a possibility for students of Dutch. She would really like to work at a publishing house, but her English is not good enough for a placement as, say, an editorial assistant at an American publishing house. She visits the placement office to ask how she can find a placement. She gets a few questions in return: is she aware of the fact that doing a placement in the United States is quite expensive? The visa alone will cost her over €840. And does she know whether the United States, like Hungary, the Czech Republic, and China, offers Dutch courses? A university offering such courses might be able to provide a starting point. Or there might be a publishing house in the Netherlands with connections in the United States; are there any Dutch novels that are translated and sold in particular states? Perhaps she could contribute to this potential market from the Netherlands – in terms of marketing, for instance? Ingrid decides to take some

> time to think about it. The advice she is given: hold on to whatever stirred your interest first: don't drop the idea and find creative ways of turning your desires into reality. And take an English course!

If the language at a placement-providing organization is different from your own and you are uncertain whether you speak that language well enough, you could take a language test at your university or other institute authorized to administer such tests. A standard English test is the Test of English as a Foreign Language (TOEFL).

Language tests for modern European languages assess the proficiency level of your writing and speaking skills in commonly known terms. To ensure consistency in their interpretation, the test results are generally described in terms laid down in the Common European Framework of Reference for Languages, or CEFR for short. It gives you an overview of the proficiency levels that you have also had to fill in on your Europass CV (see <www.internshipguide.elevenpub.com>).

5.6.2 Culture

Prepare yourself for the fact that countries where life is very different from yours also have a different *pace*. A placement assignment that can easily be rounded off in four months in the Netherlands may take you eight months in a country in Africa. You will often have to tackle logistical problems first before you get to focus on the content of your placement. An example: a student undertaking a placement at a coffee plantation in Tanzania was caught by surprise several times because the car that would drive him to the plantation every morning did not show up. The climate and the hustle and bustle of a faraway country may also prove unsettling.

If you are going to a country without being familiar with its culture, you may run the risk of experiencing culture shock. You may feel confused and lonely, have headaches or abdominal pain, experience homesickness, and be unable to feel positive about your new surroundings. These are symptoms that many students have when they go abroad on long visits and face a new environment. Expatriates may suffer from culture shock too. It's caused by not recognizing cultural expressions.

Geert Hofstede studied the way in which values in the workplace (in this particular instance, IBM) are influenced by our culture. According to Hofstede, experiences in our youth are responsible for culture shock. Our mental software contains fundamental values taught to us at a very young age. Those values are so obvious to us that we're often not even aware of them. Rituals, heroes, and symbols – our conscious, more superficial cultural expressions – are based on these values. Rituals are collective activities with no other purpose than their being performed. They can help confirm the ties in a group or the importance of a leader. Heroes are persons, living or dead, real or imagined, who have certain characteristics that are highly regarded in a culture and therefore serve as role models. Symbols are words, gestures, images, or objects that have a special meaning that can only be recognized as such by the people who share that culture. Although all these cultural expressions are visible to outsiders, the values that are attached to them are not.

The culture shock that some people experience when they spend some time in a foreign cultural environment is part of the 'acculturation curve'. This curve has a number of stages:

1. a short euphoric phase, also known as 'honeymoon';
2. a phase of culture shock, characterized by disorientation, insecurity, and loathing;
3. an acculturation phase, which sets in once the visitor has slowly learned to function under the new conditions and has adopted some of the local practices, experiences a renewed self-confidence, and becomes integrated into a new social network;
4. the mental balance phase. This stable phase can be less than, the same as, or better than the balance that the student experiences at home. According to Hofstede, if the balance is the same as at home, you are biculturally adapted. If it is better, then you have become more Roman than the Romans. It means that you have fully adapted, just like a native.

107

Sometimes the various phases follow one another in quick succession, but some phases take more time. What is the best thing to do when experiencing culture shock? If it's an acute attack of shock, it's best to find a relatively familiar, quiet place, such as a Starbucks or McDonald's. In a relatively familiar environment like that, you can recharge and prepare yourself for a new dose of stimuli. However, evading the new culture rather than accepting it is, of course, unfeasible in the long term. It may help to write down the things you find unsettling. If you read these texts over once in a while, you'll find that you get used to many of those 'strange' things quickly.

It's best to try to *prevent* a potential culture shock by getting to know the local culture. After all, once you know that Indians mean 'yes' when they shake their head and that the Chinese have no problem with spitting in public places, this will come as less of a shock. Additionally, you can try to seek contact with locals, for example by talking to native colleagues from the placement-providing organization. You can ask someone to pick you up from the airport and acquaint you with the country or region. Your host will be more than willing to tell you more about their culture. This gives you an insight into the underlying values, which helps you adjust to the host culture. With this knowledge, you may grow to accept or even appreciate the cultural differences.

5.7 Lobbying

In addition to networking and applying, there's another tool that can be used for securing your dream placement: lobbying. For a placement with one of the institutions of the European Union, for example, it is advisable to support your application with active personal lobbying.

Lobbying mainly means letting the people at your preferred organization and department know that you are applying for a placement. You can do this by giving the department manager a phone call, or by trying to make an appointment in Brussels or Strasbourg to talk about your application over a cup of coffee or lunch (at your expense). This will highlight your application, thus making you stand out from all the other applicants.

5.8 Rejection or Interview?

As you can see, you can't just sit back and wait after sending off your application letter. Still, in most cases there is nothing you can do but wait; putting too much pressure on the organization after sending your letter usually tends to be counterproductive. To keep a bit of a grip on the process, you can tell them in the last sentence of your letter that you will contact the organization within two weeks after sending it off. A sentence like that will give you the feeling of keeping some control over the procedure.

If you include such a promise in your letter, it no longer feels 'rude' to enquire about the application procedure. Do make sure you keep your promise: call them up within two weeks after sending the letter. Make sure that you get to speak to the person you directed your letter to and prepare yourself for the conversation. Ask them if you are calling at the right moment, refer to the last sentence in your letter, and ask the questions you prepared in advance. Make notes of the answers you are given, but make sure that this does not hamper the conversation. Listening carefully, responding appropriately, and asking smart questions when necessary will always be the most important things to do.

However, you usually don't have to wait two weeks for a reply when applying for a placement because the selection procedure for a placement is often much less complicated than that for a real job. It often takes no more than a few days before you receive a reply, and second interview rounds are rare. In most cases you will receive a message by phone or e-mail that the placement position is yours.

You may, of course, receive a rejection instead, for example when there are many candidates for the same placement position or when your letter or CV does not live up to the expectations of the selector or selection committee. Perhaps you lack certain important competences, or they might not be convinced of some of your qualities to perform certain set tasks. They may also have found someone else through a different route. It is quite common for the official and informal routes to cross paths this way, and apart from networking actively, there is little you can do about this. You will just have to accept your loss and invest your energy into finding another placement. Make it a point to ask for their reason for rejecting you. In many cases, it will indeed be something you can do little about; you are, for example, younger than what they have in mind for the ideal candidate. If their reason for rejecting you has to do with your letter or CV, this is also good to know because you can then improve this in future applications.

If you receive rejections on more than four placement applications, you should discuss this with your lecturer or placement coordinator. He or she can help you determine why you are turned down every time. A careers advisor may also help you with this.

109

Agreements on the placement process are often made during the placement interview, which is why the next step will discuss how placement contracts are drawn up.

Conclusion

Applying for a placement starts with collecting all relevant information about the position and the placement advertisement, but also about the application procedure and the person whom you are directing your letter to. You can do this through information that the company puts online or sends out via the press or via interviews in, for instance, company magazines, but also via the phone call you make in advance. We recommend you never send an application letter *without gaining in-depth knowledge of the addressee.*

Basically every placement provider expects you to send at least a CV when applying for a placement. In most cases, a CV is all they need, and you might be accepted on the basis of a phone call. Some placement providers also ask for a short motivational text or a letter. If it's possible, placement providers prefer to meet you in person. Only then will you be invited for an interview, so there won't always be a real interview and, therefore, a full-fledged application procedure.

There are different types of CV. Depending on the organization's requirements, you can modify your basic CV into a solicited CV or a skills CV. The requirements are always the same: a CV needs to be complete, concise, organized, clear, interesting, professional, concrete, and appropriate. It should also reflect your competences. Application letters also come in different types. A letter written in response to an advertisement can be a bit more specific than an unsolicited application letter. While most placements are found via networking and unsolicited applications, applying via an online form or an employment agency is becoming more and more common. This is especially true for placements abroad, as they involve differences in language and culture.

Always ask someone to proofread the solicited CVs and letters you draw up. Does it fit the organization? Is it not too modest? Is it not too boastful either? Ask someone who is good at editing to look for any spelling and grammar errors. Put the CV down for a few days and read it again. Make sure that the CVs you send to the organizations are the same as the ones you put on the Internet. Regularly update your LinkedIn profile.

Step 6 The Interview

Once your application letter or CV has captured the attention of one or more organizations, you have overcome the first obstacle. You have a foot in the door, but are not inside yet. The organization is not going to make any rash decisions, so the selection procedure will have to determine whether you are indeed the right person for the placement.

Once you are considered suitable, you have to submit a description of the assignment to your lecturer. After all, it can be considered a placement only if your lecturer is willing to award credits to it. You can register for your placement only once it has been approved. This means that you cannot fully commit yourself yet when negotiating your placement, and you should tell the host institution clearly that your plan has to be approved by your lecturer first.

This is a complicated process. Unlike job interviews, placement interviews often lead directly to agreements. A second application round is usually not necessary. This is why this step in drawing up a contract focuses on the interview first. The next section discusses how to get your placement approved by the department; a phase in which you are often required to negotiate. Once you have made the necessary arrangements with both your supervisors, they can be laid down in a placement contract.

Most placement interviews take no more than an hour. You usually get to talk to a selection committee of one or more persons who also speak with other candidates. The interview may also take place via telephone or webcam. Naturally, interviewing conventions differ from country to country.

As with all the previous steps in the application process, it is important to prepare yourself thoroughly for an interview. Show the selection committee that you have come prepared and that you are interested not just in the placement, but also in the company, the department, and your place within it. This shows your motivation. Moreover, a well-prepared interview will boost your confidence, which means that you can make a good impression.

6.1 Preparing for the Interview

Your preparation will largely consist of anticipating the questions that the selector or selection committee might pose to you. Know that they might base the interview not on your CV but on your profile on LinkedIn or Facebook instead; these, after all, contain your photos. Make sure the information you provide on these social networking sites doesn't differ too much from your CV. The selector will ask content-related questions in order to form a complete picture of you.

The selectors have to decide whether you are the most suitable candidate for the placement. They do this by asking themselves questions that they will be able to answer by the end of the interview, for instance:
- Does the candidate fit within our business philosophy? Is he/she proactive, innovative, reliable, capable, flexible, accurate, solution driven, and able to distinguish between main and secondary issues?
- Does the candidate demonstrate independence? Is the candidate extrovert: does he/she easily share thoughts and express feelings? Is he/she friendly? Is the candidate open-minded about different opinions and alternative solutions? Is the candidate stable enough and not easily taken aback?
- Will the candidate be able to function within the department?
- Will the candidate be pleasant to work with?

112

You may have noticed that none of the questions above are about your field of study. These may be asked, but are not the most important. After all, by mentioning your degree(s), diplomas, certificates, and experience in your letter and CV, you have already demonstrated what you are capable of.

As long as you know the answers to those questions, you can prepare for the interview. The worst thing you can do is to go to the interview unprepared, thinking: 'I can't prepare for it anyway 'cause I don't know what they're gonna ask, so I'll just see what happens.'

The selector wants to form an impression of you, and uses your CV to bring that impression to life. What kind of impression that will be is to a large extent up to you. Even though you are not in charge of the interview, a thorough preparation will give you the means to influence its content and direction; by gathering, for example, as much information as possible, knowing what your generic competences are, memorizing particular situations that *demonstrate* these competences (see Section 6.1.3), 'cleaning' your social media (see Section 6.1.4), and by making sure you wear the right clothes (see Section 6.1.5).

6.1.1   Gathering Information

In order to be able to answer the interview questions in Section 6.2, you will have to be aware of the organization's indicators; this not only goes for commercial organizations, but also for governmental organizations and NGOs. The interviewers won't expect you to carry out weeks of study on their organization, but they do expect you to demonstrate *some* knowledge of their company. Bolte's (2003) advice is to know something about:

- The number of people working within the organization; are there 15, 1,500, or 15,000 employees?
- Its main products or services.
- Its main market.
- The company's organizational structure. How many branches does the company have? Are there any international branches – for production in low-wage countries, for example? Are these subsidiaries or partners? Is it a centrally managed company or do the subsidiaries or divisions operate relatively independently?
- The main customers. Are these private consumers or large companies?
- The turnover and profit. You won't always be able to get at the exact numbers, but an indication is sufficient. An annual report might be available on the website of the Chamber of Commerce.
- The company's history. It is good to know whether it concerns a new company with mostly young people, a company formed from a recent merger, or a centuries-old company with a rich tradition.
- The competition. Whom does the organization fear? Whom does it compete with?
- The organizational culture. Is the company known for being closed, ambitious, informal, innovative? What do the employees say about this?
- Company news. What is the latest press release about? What is coming up? What are they working on? What is their latest product?

Most of this information can be found on the company's website. You could also call the company's Human Resource Management department. Tell them you are preparing for a job interview, and they'll often send you information in the form of a financial or social annual report, a newsletter, or a brochure. You can use the organization's indicators in your answers to the questions mentioned above (*e.g.* the question why you are applying to that particular company in that particular country). Do make sure that you mention the *correct and latest* numbers and news. Also make sure that you use only official information and that you know it by heart. Only then can you demonstrate that you came properly prepared.

The information you also need to have prepared for yourself mainly concerns the placement criteria. What kind of assignments am I allowed to choose for my degree programme? What is the minimum and maximum duration of the placement? Is it possible to do a part-time placement? What are my faculty's expectations regarding supervision at the placement site? Are there any forms that need to be filled in? Will I be insured during the placement? Is it possible to find accommodation near the placement-providing organization? What kind of remuneration do I have in mind? And, above all, how many days does it take for the university to give its approval? After the interview, you should meet straightaway with the person responsible for approving your placement (Board of Examiners, placement coordinator, or supervising lecturer). Placement providers do not like to be kept waiting for a decision.

Last but not least, when preparing for the interview for a placement abroad you should also focus on the country's language and culture. If you don't familiarize yourself with their rituals and organizational procedures, the application process is doomed to fail.

Manon is thrilled. With the help of the careers advisor at a faculty Career Day she finds out what kind of placement she wants to do. Although a student of Canadian Studies, she discovers that she wants to continue in her field of interest: Film. Between June and October, she contacts all major film agencies in the Netherlands in search of a placement opportunity. She hits the mark in Rotterdam: production company FilmA would gladly have her for three months and would allow her to participate in all daily activities. She enthusiastically tells the placement coordinator about the placement. The placement coordinator asks her what kind of assignment they will give her. 'Well, that's kinda hard to say,' Manon replies. 'They haven't really said. It's more like an observational placement.' She wonders if she will get her professor's approval in time; after all, the placement starts in only three days and she has not yet been able to contact him. She also wants to know how she should plan the placement to prevent study delay. It's 26 October today, the placement starts on 1 November, and her enrolment at the university will be terminated at the end of January. She'd rather not reregister after January because that would mean she'd have to borrow extra money. Moreover, if she were to reregister she would have to pay tuition fees again. The placement coordinator asks her why it took her so long to notify her of her plans. Manon replies that arranging the placement went very quickly. She was told that she could start straightaway and has no problems with that. But there's something she wants to ask the placement coordinator: 'Is it possible to graduate during the placement period?' After some calculating, the placement coordinator comes to the conclusion that, formally, it's possible. The number of credits allocated to placements in her degree programme

> equals 280 hours, or seven 40-hour weeks. If she starts on 1 November, she'll have spent the required hours on placement by 20 December. If she can have her placement report approved by her professor in the week after, she should be able to apply for her degree certificate before the end of the year. If, after that, she should wish to continue working at FilmA, that would be up to her. The credits would still be awarded to her, the placement would still be on her certificate, and she wouldn't need to reregister at university. What would be the wisest thing to do? Against her usual judgement, the placement coordinator advises Manon to undertake the placement in her own time. It's very unlikely that she gets her professor to approve the placement within three days. There's a lot of pressure, the placement assignment hasn't been formulated yet, and her professor wouldn't approve an observational placement for her Master's degree programme. Instead, she could undertake the placement as work (voluntary or paid), and a future employer would appreciate an initiative like this as much as he would a placement on her certificate. In the end, it's the experience that counts. Manon says she doesn't really need the credits because she's already earned sufficient credits with subsidiary subjects. She decides to carry out the assignment as an employee.

Applicants will rarely be asked to produce their degree certificates or lists of marks. Information that may spark a selection committee's interest instead is the 'evidence' of your experience. If there are any relevant articles you have written or particular certificates you have earned, take these with you in a tidy folder. When asked for any of those documents, you can pull out your folder and present it.

6.1.2   Generic Competences

Presenting information alone is not enough. The placement provider will not only try to assess your level of knowledge, he or she will also want to find out more about your social intelligence. Apart from focusing on the content when preparing for an interview, you also have to focus on the presentation. After all, first impressions are not based on clever answers, but on the way you shake the interviewer's hand and the way you react when you're asked how your trip went.

Keep in mind that the interviewer has to form an opinion of you in a short time. Everything you say or do will be taken into account. The way you smile, the way you sit, how frequently you seek eye contact; all this information is crucial. How do you respond to their questions? Do you ask for an explanation when something is unclear to you? This shows the interviewer whether or not you have an open character, are strong, stress-resilient, eager to work hard, willing to take initiatives, are a go-getter and/or can cooperate – in short, whether or not you can carry out the placement assignment with minimal supervision. When the interview takes place over the telephone, your pace and voice will help shape the impression they have of you.

6.1.3   The STAR Method

Personality is the most important quality that employers base their selection on in job interviews, followed by flexibility, social competence, suitability, and, lastly, appearance. In placement interviews too you may notice that the selection committee pays a lot of attention to your suitability for the organization, more so than to your ability to carry out the placement. The reason for this is that placements are often seen as a *recruitment tool* – a way to tap into new talent. Finding new employees through recruitment and selection agencies or advertising is, after all, an expensive and time-consuming activity, and a placement can serve as the perfect trial period. Have a look at the websites of large multinationals or EU institutions, for instance. In the 'working for Shell' section, placements are listed as the third option. An enquiry among graduates supports this assumption: no less than one-third of students who have undertaken a placement say that their first job after graduation was offered to them by their placement provider.

Once you know that placements are used as a recruitment tool, it should come as no surprise when no mention is made of the placement assignment. The interview may be focused entirely on your abilities, which would make it an asymmetrical interview. The selector or selection committee would be asking you quite a few questions, but content-related questions on your part would get little response. Your discussion partner would decide on the topics of conversation and there'd be nothing you could do but go along with it. This can give you a sense of powerlessness.

Step 2 showed that describing your generic competences may help to make a good impression. Another method to help you get a firmer grip on the conversation is the 'STAR method'. This method is often used by interviewers and consists of asking you for concrete examples of the experiences in your CV. 'STAR' stands for Situation, Task, Action, Result.

To prepare for this method you have to memorize concrete examples from your recent past that are related to the key competences required for the placement. Think of one situation per competence, and for each situation think of the tasks, actions, and the result (see the box for an example). Limit yourself to a maximum of five competences (and therefore five situations). By practising these sets out loud with someone, you put them 'in your hat', as it were. You can then 'pull them out of your hat' during the interview when asked for it or whenever you think it appropriate. Just like preparing examples of your generic competences, using the STAR method can give you more control over the conversation.

Example

The placement-providing organization is looking for someone who is stress-resilient. You expect the selection committee to ask for an example that shows you possess this particular quality. Your CV mentions, among other things, your membership of the board of your study association.

Situation

Try to think of a concrete situation in which you proved to be stress-resilient. You may remember, for instance, the pressure you felt when the board of your study association had two months to organize a Career Event for all your fellow students, with a celebrity on the list of speakers as well as a renowned professor and a number of successful alumni. When, three weeks before the event, the church building you had hired turned out to be double-booked, you remained calm and moved the event to a different, equally suitable venue.

Task

Try to remember precisely what your tasks were in that stressful situation. You were the chairperson, which means you chaired the meetings and had to try to hold the board together amidst the chaos. The invitations referring to the original venue had already been printed and were ready to be sent. Explain how, together with the PR commissioner, you managed to arrange new invitations within a day.

Action

Tell the selection committee how you prevented the board from having to pay for the invitations twice. Describe how you got the council of the double-booked church to pay for the revised invitations.

Result

Tell them about the results. Describe how great it felt that, under your leadership, a close-knit team was formed that overcame all setbacks quickly and professionally. Nobody, apart from the printer and the church treasurer, was aware that the invitations that were sent out the following day were reprints. If anyone complimented you on keeping your head cool like that, do mention this.

Reflection

A question that may follow is whether you would do it differently next time. In what way did this experience lead to n ew insights and behaviour? A possible answer is that next time you will make sure that the contract includes a confirmation of your booking. Employers like hearing that you *learn* consciously.

117

6.1.4 Social Media

One aspect of your preparation that you may not have considered concerns social media. Your profile on LinkedIn, your second life on Facebook, your tweets, or your blogs and messages on other social networking sites might reveal more about you to your placement provider than you might wish. Once messages and pictures have been posted they are difficult to remove, so you'd better bear this in mind as soon as you begin your studies. This means you should not post comments without thinking, or only do so using a pseudonym.

Images are powerful: if the selection committee sees a silly picture of you on the Internet before the interview, you have already made a first impression. A picture of you standing drunk on a beach reduces your chances of being considered a serious candidate. You will need to reverse that image of you as a layabout. *If* you get that chance, that is; a picture like that is often reason enough not to invite candidates for an interview.

You should also realize that the person doing the appointing will often be older than you. Someone of an older generation might not always be willing to place whatever you put online into perspective. He or she may not understand the entertainment value (or use) of the Internet.

6.1.5 Clothing

An important question that many applicants face is: what to wear? You should address this question at least a week before the interview; this gives you time to go shopping for things you still need. Bear in mind that it is best to dress 'smartly'. Do not go to the interview dressed in a T-shirt and jeans, even if the atmosphere at the placement-providing organization is rather informal. Your clothes do not necessarily have to conform to the latest fashion, but a suit bought a couple of years ago may be worn out.

Also, some research into company conventions may be useful. Do most employees wear jackets? And do the women wear skirt suits? Dress accordingly. A rule of thumb is not to wear anything distracting. It's better to be overdressed than underdressed. Do the employees dress casually and are suits the exception rather than the rule? Wear a smart jacket with a shirt and matching trousers or skirt. Whatever you decide to wear, make sure your clothes fit comfortably. That is why you should wear your new clothes at least once before wearing them to an interview – they will fit better.

A useful tip: contrasting combinations, such as a dark blue jacket and a white shirt, radiate authority. This makes you appear stand-offish. Choose less contrasting combinations if you want to appear more approachable.

6.2   The Interview

Most placement interviews are conducted by three people at the most:
1. the manager of the department offering the placement position (who is often also to be your supervisor);
2. a future colleague;
3. a personnel officer (of the HRM department).

Whether you are faced with one person or three, their mission is the same: to judge whether you are the most suitable candidate for the placement on offer. In addition to that, the colleague will want to know if you are pleasant to work with.

Selectors will approach you as an equal, so behave like one. If you are still a student this may seem difficult, but you'll just have to try. Keep in mind that you are not the only one who benefits from a positive outcome of the interview: the organization invests time and energy in you because you offer something they want: your commitment. The easiest thing to do, therefore, is to just be yourself. Try to act naturally, as if you were with friends or family. If you are nervous, it is perfectly okay to tell them this. It may bring you relief and break the ice, and the selector cannot help but appreciate your honesty.

General points of advice:
*   Be on time. Make sure that you know where you have to be; arrive five to ten minutes early. It gives you time to take in your surroundings and to check yourself in the bathroom mirror (and give yourself a pep talk ;-)).
*   Do not drink any alcohol the night before the interview and do not eat too much garlic or strong spices. Smells, too, are part of the impression you make.
*   Practise the interview.
*   Show initiative and radiate enthusiasm.
*   Relate, where possible, your knowledge, skills, and personality to the position. Give examples of your abilities where possible. Elaborate on your strengths, but do not pretend to have nothing but good qualities.
*   Talk about your negative qualities only when prompted. Do not dwell on them and try to give them a positive twist. Do not be negative about matters in your past or present. Speak the truth, and do not be arrogant or indifferent.

An interview may go as follows:

Welcome and Introduction

Whoever leads the conversation will usually welcome you in the waiting space. When they come to fetch you, they welcome you and introduce themselves with a handshake. Perhaps they introduce the other selector (or selectors) to you. They then tell you where you can sit and will often ask if you want something to drink. Accepting the offer is often appreciated (turning it down is even considered rude in some countries).

Try to be as calm as possible when entering the room. Slow down your pace, relax your shoulders, and give everyone present a firm handshake while look-ing them in the eyes. It is part of the ritual of interviewing for the selection committee to try to put you at ease. Always respond to the selector's small talk; a conversation about trivial matters is decisive for the first impression you make. If they do not ask you anything, for example because your interview is one of many in a row, you should make a casual remark yourself. Say something about the building, for example, or about a painting, or the view. The selection committee will consider such a comment as a pleasant interlude, and will start the interview in a relaxed manner. Then again, this may vary from culture to culture.

Opening

The person who leads the interview gives an introductory talk to put you at ease and to let you get accustomed to the room and your interviewers. He or she also tells you how they want to conduct the interview and what steps are to follow. Your CV will in most cases form the basis for the interview; then again, it could just as easily be based on your LinkedIn profile.

Anything could be the topic of conversation during the introduction, such as your trip, your degree programme, company information, the department, or the placement. They might tell you that you can always ask questions or ask for an explanation, or that they will ask you questions and/or present you with a case. They may also tell you how long the interview is expected to take, or discuss the application process and tell you when and how you will hear about the outcome.

Body

The body of the interview contains the questions and cases. Do not answer with just a 'yes' or 'no', but explain your answers. It is not an oral exam, but a conversation in which you present yourself. Ask the interviewer to repeat or clarify the question if there is something you don't understand. If you're not sure whether your response was clear enough, you can ask them if it answers their question or if they will allow you to clarify your answer. Also keep an eye on the interviewer's non-verbal expressions and adapt your contribution to the conversation accordingly.

121

In this phase of the interview, the selection committee will be paying close attention to you to see if you are the most suitable candidate. Selectors will often try to find out how you react to unexpected situations. Consequently, you never know in advance how an interview will *really* go. If the placement requires a proficiency in English, do not be surprised when they switch to English halfway through the interview. If you have been expecting questions only, do not be surprised when the selection committee suddenly presents you with a practical case. This will be discussed in further detail later in this chapter.

Conclusion

Sometimes the final phase contains a summary of the interview, and the candidate is given a final opportunity to ask questions or make comments. What often happens next is that the participants express their appreciation for the interview. Sometimes the interviewer will repeat what steps are to follow. Finally, the selection committee takes leave of the candidate.

In case it has *not* been addressed yet, it is common practice at this point to ask how the application process will proceed. How many candidates are applying for the placement? When will you hear about the outcome of the interview?

While the interview itself is at an end, this is an important moment. You now have to explain to them how the procedure continues at your university. Do you meet the entry requirements for the placement? Do you need permission from a study coordinator? When will you know whether you can start?

If the application procedure consists of just the one interview, then this is also the moment to ask about a potential remuneration. This will be discussed in the section below.

Sections 6.2.1 and 6.2.2 give an overview of two types of questions you may get; it gives you a better idea of how an interview may go. This is followed by two example cases and other tricks you might be faced with. More information can be found in the instructor's manual at <www.internshipguide.elevenpub.com>.

6.2.1 Questions about the Organization

During the interview you may expect questions about the organization, such as:

Why do you want to do your placement at this particular organization?
What do you know about our organization? Why do you want to do your placement here?
What can you contribute to our organization? Why do you think you are suitable for this placement with this organization?
What aspects of the placement appeal to you and what appeals to you less? Why?
What would be your dream placement?
Why would we hire you?
What do you expect from a placement in general, and what do you expect from this particular placement?
What kind of assignment would you be able to do?
How much time do you think you need to be able to carry out the assignment?
When can you begin?
How many days per week are you available?

The lecturer's guide that comes with this book provides possible answers to these questions.

6.2.2 Questions about Yourself

You can also expect questions about yourself, such as:

Tell us something about yourself.
What do you like about your degree programme? What do you like less?
What are your strengths and weaknesses?
Which quality would you like to develop further?
Can you give examples of how you have shown initiative?
Why have you done so many – or so few – different things?
Who or what has influenced your life?
How do you define 'success'?
What problems did you face in your life and how did you solve them?
Is this the kind of work you really want to do?
What do you expect from supervision?
What kind of colleague will you be?
How do you see your future in five years' time? What do you aim for in your career?
Is there anything you want to ask us?

6.2.3   Remuneration

Many countries have hardly any or no legislation when it comes to placements. The legal right to a remuneration often does not exist. In general, a remuneration is regarded as an expense allowance, which has to be agreed upon between the student and the placement provider or between the university and the placement provider. Remunerations are therefore not compulsory, and neither is there a minimum remuneration.

What do you want to earn? Would you settle for less?
You probably know from the interview or advertisement whether a remuneration is available. If this was a prerequisite for you to do the placement, it's often too late to start negotiations about this now. However, it's not yet too late to discuss the exact amount of the fee.

What do you value more: money or type of work?
Type of work, of course – but, unfortunately, you don't get something for nothing. Always be open about the *reason* you are enquiring about a remuneration. You have to quit your part-time job in order to be able to do the placement, for instance, or you have to rent a more expensive room near the placement-providing company. Just be honest, and tell them that it is very hard for you to do the placement without a remuneration. If it's really urgent, for example because you want to go to an expensive foreign city, make sure you set a budget beforehand.

If you manage to negotiate remuneration successfully, make sure it is laid down in the placement contract.

6.2.4   Interview for a Placement Abroad

Step 1 has discussed the advantages of a placement in another country. Content-wise, a placement abroad doesn't have to differ all that much from a placement at home. The methods of applying, however, may differ considerably – not only where it concerns the means with which to conduct the interview, but also when it comes to the approach.

An advantage of an international job interview is that you don't have to worry too much about what to wear, as such interviews usually take place over the phone. Only when doing the interview via Skype or some other Voice over IP tool do your looks, the lighting, and the background matter. Selectors will only very occasionally travel to your country to recruit students on placement. This is sometimes done for placements with embassies or consulates, for instance. One of the drawbacks of doing the interview over the phone is that your language proficiency might play a bigger role than your CV. Another drawback is that you miss the non-verbal communication to which you could adapt your contribution.

Information on applying in EU countries can be found in the booklet *You will hear from us . . .: What you should know when applying for a job in another EEA country* by EURES. It can be ordered free or downloaded in various languages via the website of the European Commission (see <www.internshipguide. elevenpub.com>).

6.2.5   Applying with a Performance Disability

Perhaps you have a performance disability and are applying for a placement position. Performance disabilities and chronic illnesses include any physical, sensory, or other functional disorders that cause delay in completing your degree. This could be a physical disability, a chronic illness, or psychological problems, but also autism or dyslexia. You've probably had to talk about your disability before, for instance when you needed to make use of the facilities your university provides for disabled students. You are now facing a dilemma: whether to mention your disability in the interview or not.

Perhaps you'd rather keep it quiet, and this is sometimes perfectly okay. If, for example, you are applying for a part-time placement and your asthma prevents you from working more than 5 hours a day, you might plan your days in such a way that you won't have to work more than that. Neither do you have to mention any long-term illnesses in your past. And if your disability does not hamper your performance in any way, there's no need to refer to it either, of course.

In most other cases, however, it is advisable to talk about your performance disability, as long as you mention it at the right moment. That is, at a later stage of the interview. By then, you have hopefully already convinced the selection committee of your suitability. They will be enthusiastic about your qualifications, experience, and personality. Or, in AIDA terms, you will have caught their *Attention*, you will have raised their *Interest*, they will *Desire* what you may contribute, and they are about to take *Action* by selecting you. If they are willing to give you a chance, it will be easier for you to mention your disability. The rest of the interview can then be dedicated to the things you *can* do. You can provide examples of what you have achieved, and perhaps explain that your disability has made you very persevering or helped you develop other qualities.

6.2.6 Unexpected Questions

This chapter has already mentioned some of the questions that can be expected in an interview. It speaks for itself that a company that, say, organizes large dance and music events may, in addition to the usual questions, ask you about a particular festival or your favourite music. When you are applying to a current affairs programme for TV, you can expect questions about the news of the day and how you would turn that news into an item for that programme. And when applying for a placement at a museum, you can expect them to ask which museums you like to visit and which artists appeal to you specifically. But what to do when they suddenly pose you an entirely different question or a problem that they want you to solve? This section will discuss unexpected *odd questions*, unexpected *impertinent questions*, unexpected cases, and unexpected language switching.

Odd Questions

Generally, unexpected interview questions are, as the name suggests, difficult to prepare for. Sometimes, the selector may unexpectedly ask you an odd question, such as 'What would you do with a million ping-pong balls?' (to test your creativity) or 'How many museums does New York have?' (to test your analytical skills). You may feel like you are being mocked, especially if you did not see the question coming. You could ask them why they are asking you this, or give an equally odd answer. There are no right or wrong answers to odd questions. They just want to see whether you are caught off balance by an unexpected situation, how you cope with that situation, and whether you can think outside the box. The best thing to do is to remain calm; do not get agitated, and give an answer that suits you or is topical.

Impertinent Questions

Some questions can be considered impertinent; this differs from country to country. 'Are you living with someone?' for example, or 'Do you want children?' or 'Are you religious?' Or a question about your sexual orientation disguised in the question, 'If we were to call your partner, what would (s)he say about you?' Or questions about your physical health while it is not really relevant to the placement itself: 'Are you ill often?' 'Do you take any medication and, if you do, for what?' or 'Are you pregnant?' You don't have to answer such questions and they are even forbidden by law because they may lead to discrimination. The Equal Opportunities Acts prohibits employers from discriminating on the basis of religion, political affiliation, life philosophy, race, gender, nationality, sexual orientation, or marital status. In addition to such laws, various countries have a 'recruitment code' that can help you prepare for the interview. What to do if they ask you an impertinent question anyway? What do you reply? Remain polite; the answer 'that's private' should suffice. The moment you are faced with such a question, you will realize that the fact that they are asking you that question tells you a lot about the selector and, therefore, about the organization. The selector is not the only one who has to make a choice; you, too, have to decide: do you really want to do your placement there?

Cases

Imagine you are applying for a placement that requires you to interview company staff. The topic of the assignment is the company's internal communication. The selection committee will want to know whether you can deal with people who are reluctant to participate in such an interview. It is quite possible that they want to try this out on you by presenting you with a case involving such a reluctant employee. You will be given a scenario where you introduce yourself and are getting ready to start with the interview, with the interviewee then refusing to answer your questions. As you did not prepare this case beforehand, you will have to improvise an answer to the question 'What would you do?' You'll have to use your imagination, especially if you have little experience with situations like this. First you have to make sure that you fully understand the situation. Ask for clarification, and, if you still don't understand, be honest and tell them so. If you've never been in such a situation, you should not just make something up. Instead, you can say that you have been in a situation similar to this. Ask the selection committee if you can describe it to them, and give a clear, step-by-step description of what you did back then. You can use the STAR method for this (as discussed in Section 6.1.3) or an example you prepared for one of your generic competences.

Doing the Interview in Another Language

If the placement advertisement asks for an active command of a particular foreign language, don't be surprised when the interviewers suddenly switch to that language. The idea is that you switch to that language too and that you continue the conversation smoothly. It's okay if you do not immediately come up with the words or stammer a bit now and then. It is about showing them that you are not afraid to speak in a foreign language and that you can get by in everyday situations. Everyone knows that spending an extended period in a foreign-language environment will automatically improve your proficiency in that language. Tell them, if necessary, that you are willing to do an advanced language course prior to the placement.

6.2.7 Psychological Assessment

Organizations have an interest in students who stay on at the company after their placement ends, which is why a psychological assessment may be part of the application procedure. It's a time-consuming method, and therefore quite expensive. Students can do such a test only if the placement is approved by their lecturer.

Such a test may seem a bit over the top for a placement of only three or four months, but it does tell you something about the time and effort the selectors invest in their assessment of you as a serious potential colleague. Perhaps to your surprise, the placement assignment itself is often not the first, but the second item on the agenda – before discussing the work you could be doing, the selection committee will first want to get to know you.

The aim of psychological evaluation is to find out whether you are truly suitable for the placement and the organization. It gives employers an extra sense of security because in interviews, candidates may pretend to be someone they're not. This type of assessment is usually outsourced to an independent agency; only large (government) organizations have their own testing department.

A psychological evaluation usually consists of an oral and written test. In the oral test, a psychologist asks you questions about your motives for applying and the expectations you have of the placement. Sometimes the psychologist discusses the written test as well, in which case he or she examines whether the test results match your behaviour. It is hardly possible to practise for the oral test, but it *is* possible to practise for the written test online in order to improve your testing skills and, more importantly, to help you get a grip on your nerves.

6.2.8   Assessment

The *selection assessment* is a means to find out how you would behave in a particular situation. In an assessment centre, you are confronted with 'real-life' situations that may also occur on placement. This method, too, is used only when your placement has been approved by your lecturer.

The assessment can come in the form of an individual assignment (a presentation or role), a dialogue (*e.g.* where you have to try to extract information from some-one), or a group assignment (*e.g.* a discussion). The assignments are based on the qualities that are important for the placement. Is it important, for instance, that you are stress-resilient? Then this is where you have to show that you are. Experi-enced assessors will then determine on the basis of fixed criteria whether you can cope with the simulated situation. As this is an expensive research method (often outsourced to an external agency, too), it is not a regular component of placement application procedures. You can prepare for it as for an interview – by collecting a lot of information about the host organization, but also by reading books on management skills, and by working on your social skills at a special training centre or online.

Participants in these tests have rights too, and you should be aware of them. For instance, the assessors should tell you in advance what the testing day is going to be like and how the results are made known. The report will usually go to you first, so that you can give permission to have it sent to the placement provider. The psy-chologist will at some point have to discuss the results with you. You can then ask him or her what advice was formed (on the basis of the results) and released to the placement-providing organization. The placement provider is allowed to store the results, but needs your consent to use them for other purposes. If you don't want that, or if you didn't get accepted for the placement, you can ask the organization to destroy them.

Conclusion

The application procedure for placements usually involves just one interview, which is conducted face-to-face or – for placements abroad – by telephone or via the Internet. The interview may be carried out by more than one person. Your CV or LinkedIn profile often serves as a guideline, and thorough preparation can exercise considerable influence on the outcome. Knowledge of the country's culture, of the organization, and of your own strengths and weaknesses are the most useful (see generic competences in Section 2.2.1 (Step 2) and the STAR method in Section 6.1.3). Once you realize that it is not only you who benefit from the placement but that *you are also an asset* to the placement-providing organization, you are ready to meet your interviewers as equals. The more relaxed you are, the better. It also enables you to respond properly to cases, unexpected questions, and language switching. It's perfectly normal and okay in some countries to ask questions yourself. At the end of the interview, do not be afraid to ask about the steps that are to follow and the possibilities of remuneration. The application procedure may include a psychological evaluation or assessment. The next step addresses the formalities you have to take care of once you are accepted for a placement.

Step 7 The Placement

When you've applied successfully, you will have to request approval for the *content* of the placement – that is, if you want to earn credits for it. This is often done by drawing up a placement plan. Once the placement is approved and you have been appointed a supervising lecturer, you can fill in the placement contract. The contract lays down the requirements that should be met in order to earn credits for the placement. Once the contract has been signed by all parties involved, the placement can get started.

From the preparation phase onwards, you are going to have to manoeuvre back and forth between your university and the placement-providing organization. Many students see finalizing the arrangements of their placement as navigating between Scylla and Charybdis:

> In Homer's epic poem the *Odyssey*, Odysseus, King of Ithaca, is on his way home after the Trojan War. On his journey he faces many obstacles. One of the dangers he has to overcome is Scylla and Charybdis. Scylla is a sea monster with six heads and twelve legs. Her sister Charybdis is an enormous whirlpool. They live opposite each other in a narrow channel of water (the Strait of Messina). On his way to Ithaca, Odysseus cannot simply avoid them both. The sisters are so close together that if you were to try to avoid one of the monsters, it would be near impossible not to fall prey to the other. In the end, Odysseus survives them both, and, with the help of the goddess, Athena, he manages to return to his wife and subjects.

Navigating between your placement provider and your university is a bit like steering into the Strait of Messina. The only difference is that they are not out to devour you, nor do they have conflicting interests. Both want to work towards a meaningful, interesting placement for you.

This chapter addresses the formal aspects that may play a role in the placement itself.

7.1 The Placement Assignment

If the placement-providing organization wants to hire you as a student on placement, you have to discuss the content of the placement with the supervising lecturer or the Board of Examiners. First, however, you have to know what the placement assignment is. If the host institution wants to take you on, but they do not yet know which tasks to give you, you'll need to work on that first. The placement-providing organization is primarily responsible for formulating the placement assignment. It is important that the host institution have an *interest* in your assignment; otherwise, your work will disappear in a drawer as soon as you have left. That's hardly motivating.

If the host institution or your contact person does not really know about possible placement assignments or if there is more than one project that your placement could be linked to, you could propose ideas for an assignment yourself. Your lecturer can give you examples of placement assignments, or you can ask senior students about theirs. You can often also consult placements reports of other students (see Section 3.1). You will learn that no placement is the same, if only because of the additional tasks that may be carried out in addition to the assignment itself. An exact example of your placement may therefore not be found. In such a case, you have to come up with an assignment together with your placement provider.

7.2 Approval for Your Placement: Placement Plan

You should already have notified your faculty of the fact that you want to do a placement. Perhaps you need to ask for approval via a special form, for example because certain criteria must be met before you can enter the placement phase. You may need to pass a particular course first, for instance, or earn a fixed number of credits.

If you have met these conditions, then the placement assignment needs to be approved. After all, in order to qualify for credits, the placement has to meet the criteria set by the degree programme. The lecturer or Board of Examiners decides whether the placement you found meets these criteria. While this can be done in a face-to-face consultation, it is often done by means of a placement plan drawn up by the student. Some faculties provide a standard form for this. If this is not the case, you will need to draw up a plan yourself.

A placement plan consists of the following core components:
- the student's details (name, student number, degree programme, address, place of residence, e-mail address, mobile telephone number);
- details of the supervising lecturer (name, degree programme, e-mail address, telephone number);
- details of the host institution (name of organization, address, city);
- details of the host institution supervisor (name, position, e-mail address, and direct telephone number);
- brief description of the organization and/or sector to which the host institution belongs;
- length of the placement and when it takes place, plus the number of hours of work per day/week;
- description of the placement assignment/content of the placement;
- time schedule of the specific tasks that will be carried out in the placement period (including any tasks that are not assignment-related);
- learning outcomes and competences to be achieved;
- nature and frequency of supervision by the placement provider;
- nature and frequency of supervision by the lecturer.

An example of a placement plan can be found on <www.internshipguide.elevenpub.com>.

Arnold goes to the placement office because he has a question. He says that he 'is required to do a placement', and that he has come up with something. He plays in a band that will soon be recording an album at a production company in Rotterdam, and he would like to do his placement there. The manager of the company is open to this idea. Arnold would now like to know what the placement requirements are and whether his idea is feasible. He is a student of Culture and Media specializing in Music. A placement at a music or production company is therefore a viable option, provided the placement provider (the production house) is able to appoint a supervisor for the academic placement. Arnold should also have his own (temporary) workstation with a PC so that he can work on the assignment independently. In addition, the assignment should contain at least two months of full-time work that ties in with the degree programme and is challenging enough to stimulate Arnold's creativity and intelligence. He can put these matters on paper in a placement plan, including possible start and end dates, and submit it to the lecturer for approval. Arnold can only take up this placement in his degree programme and earn credits for it if he gets approval. He would be killing two birds with one stone: he'd carry out the compulsory placement programme and, indirectly, he'd be helping out his band.

In many cases, the lecturer confirms his or her approval by signing the placement plan. The lecturer may take the following points into consideration when assessing the placement or placement assignment:

- Does the placement meet the practical-supervision and workplace criteria?
- Do the placement assignment and its related tasks tie in with the degree programme's learning outcomes?
- Does the placement assignment correspond with the level of the student's degree programme?
- Is the length of the placement in accordance with the requirements?
- Are the phasing and planning of the tasks to be performed realistic?
- Are the competences to be acquired clearly and correctly formulated?
- Is it clear what the output of the placement will be?
- Is there a link to the final degree project (thesis or final-year project)?
- Is it clear what the deadline for the report will be?

Only after having received approval from your lecturer may you let the placement provider know that the placement can go ahead.

7.2.1   The Placement's Position

Not only is approval for the placement based on its content, but you also need to discuss the placement's *position within the curriculum* with your lecturer. It might be an idea to schedule the placement as the final course. After all, placements are not only a good way of exploring your career prospects because they offer a valuable insight into what you would like to do with your degree, but they have also proved useful in improving students' chances of getting a job. In some European countries, no less than 30% of students on placement are offered to work for their placement provider after their placement is over.

7.2.2   Duration of the Placement

In addition to its position in your curriculum, the *length* of your placement will also be assessed. The number of credits that are listed for the placement in your course catalogue determines the number of hours the placement has to be. In the Netherlands, for example, 1 ECTS equals 28 hours. This means that if a placement in the Netherlands is listed as 15 ECTS, it has to consist of at least 420 hours. This would correspond to a total of 10.5 weeks. Your department might accept placements that take longer than the required number of hours, though. This has to do with the market: many companies consider a two- or three-month placement to be too short. They don't mind showing a student the ropes for a couple of weeks, but they also want to profit from this investment for at least two months.

You can either continue to search for a placement that does cover the required number of hours, or you can do the following to prevent any or too much delay:

• Turn it into a part-time placement. If you know the number of credits, you can calculate the number of weeks your placement has to cover if you were to work only, say, four days a week. It is best if your placement covers at least three days a week so that it does not lose the effect of a realistic work experience.

• Plan your placement in the summer period. The advantage is that you won't miss any classes and that you can include your vacation period in the placement. It can be a few weeks longer that way, which means you will gain more experience. Another advantage is that many of your colleagues will be on holiday in the summer period, which means you may be given more responsibility. Your practical supervisor may be away for a while too, though. In that case, make sure he or she is replaced by a competent second supervisor. If your lecturer is absent, you should make arrangements too, for example if you are planning to graduate at the end of summer.

• You could break up your placement into a compulsory and a voluntary part. If you want to graduate before 1 September but your placement provider asks you to stay on after that, you could try to arrange with your lecturer to end the placement contractually within that academic year. The placement may still continue after that, but it is not the lecturer's concern because it falls outside the contract period and the lecturer's supervision, and doesn't have to be included in the placement report. You would undertake the second part of your placement on your own as 'volunteer work'. That way, you could graduate in time and avoid any additional study costs – *and* you would gain extra experience, of course. On the other hand, you wouldn't be able to enter the labour market during that period, nor would you be able to apply for benefit in most cases. Also be sure to change your insurance accordingly.

> For his degree programme in Film Studies, Thomas managed to find a placement with a film festival in Bologna. Because placements carry 10 ECTS (credits), he has to spend at least 280 hours on placement. This equals seven full-time working weeks. His placement begins on 5 July and ends on 29 August, thus lasting exactly eight weeks. Thomas has agreed to send the lecturer his placement report by e-mail on 29 August so that the lecturer can mark it right away. This way, he will receive his mark just in time to be able to graduate on 1 September. Thomas has also arranged with the organization of the film festival to stay on until January, thus gaining six months of work experience without having to suffer any delay.

7.2.3   Final-Year Project

If you want to combine your placement with your dissertation or thesis, you will have to make additional arrangements with your lecturer. For students of some degree programmes, this combination, a 'final-year project', is compulsory. Some students see the combination of placement and thesis as the ideal solution to a potential delay caused by a placement taking too long. But be warned: preparing for a final-year project takes time. Bad planning may turn a final-year project into the *cause* for study completion delay. Placement criteria are, after all, very different from those of a thesis. Combining a practical component with research, both of which have to result in a report, requires careful preparation and a tight schedule. You should therefore take a longer approval period into account, and you shouldn't wait too long before expressing your wishes to your study advisor or anyone else in charge within your degree programme. Also, don't wait too long with the formulation of your problem definition.

Once you get approval, make proper arrangements for the planning and supervision of the two components, as well as about the manner in which they will be rounded off. You should also make proper arrangements with your placement provider. If you're going to write your thesis at the placement site, it has to be crystal clear when you will be there as a student on placement and when as a researcher. It requires a certain degree of assertiveness not to respond to requests for help from your colleagues on days that you are working on your thesis. You could do your placement first, in preparation for your thesis. You could also do your research first and finish your thesis before working exclusively on your placement. Or will you be a student on placement on Mondays, Tuesdays, and Thursdays, and thesis writer on Wednesdays and Fridays?

7.2.4   'Volunteer' Placements

In this book, a 'volunteer placement' is a placement that carries no credits. Such a placement is carried out as 'volunteer work'. Although this book is limited to placements that

are awarded with credits, a placement without credits can, of course, provide you with experience too. A word of warning, though: there's no supervising lecturer involved in volunteer placements, so there's no external supervision on the content. If your colleagues keep asking you to make photocopies or to bring them coffee, it is up to you to make a stand. Many placement-providing organizations and companies, however, only hire students who undertake a placement *as part of their degree programme*. This means you have to prove that you are registered for a degree programme.

7.3 Placement Supervision

Placements that are awarded with credits are supervised by a lecturer. This supervision often takes place at a distance. Daily supervision is carried out by an employee of the host institution. During the planning phase (Section 7.2), you should agree with both your supervising lecturer and the practical supervisor on the frequency and timing of the supervision. These agreements are set down in the placement contract, which will be discussed in Section 7.4.

7.3.1   Supervision by the Lecturer

Standard supervision by the lecturer often involves at least three supervision sessions:
1. approval of the placement plan (see Section 7.1);
2. interim evaluation;
3. final evaluation and placement assessment.

If you have certain expectations regarding the degree of supervision by your lecturer, let the person in question know in advance to avoid disappointment later.

Interim Evaluation

Students are the 'project managers' of their placement. It is convenient for the supervising lecturer to let the student initiate the planning of the interim evaluation. The student can ask the lecturer to get in touch with the practical supervisor sometime halfway through the placement. However, it is the lecturer's duty to get in touch if the student fails to do this.

It's best if the lecturer contacts the host institution at the start of the placement to get to know the company and to briefly discuss the placement assignment and planning. They should get in touch again halfway through the placement, this time for the interim evaluation. Active participation by the lecturer is very much appreciated by students as well as placement providers. Also, contact with the host institution might be interesting for lecturers with an eye to placing new students on placement, increasing opportunities for graduates, and measuring degree programmes against labour-market demand. Placement providers sometimes count on visits from a lecturer. If it's not possible to visit, the meeting may also take place via telephone, Skype, or e-mail. The student can discuss this in advance.

The interim evaluation may include the following questions:
- How is the placement going so far?
  - What is going well?
  - Are there any problems (*e.g.* anything planning-related)?
- How can these problems be solved in order for the placement to be rounded off successfully?
- Has the student gained sufficient insight into the organization and the department?
- Do the student's knowledge and skills tie in with the tasks?
- Has the student achieved the learning outcomes that he planned for by now?
- Does the placement supervisor have any wishes regarding the rest of the placement? Can they be achieved within the remaining time?

- What are the plans for further supervision and for handing in the placement report (deadline)?
- Does the student receive adequate supervision?
- Does the placement live up to the student's expectations? Is it a big enough challenge?
- Are there any additional tasks/projects to which the student wants to make a contribution?

If it turns out that the placement is not proceeding according to plan, the lecturer may request an extra meeting with the practical supervisor, preferably with the student present. The placement assignment can still be adjusted at this point to enable a successful completion of the placement.

Final Evaluation

As for the interim evaluation, the student can also initiate the final evaluation. Both placement supervisors may conduct the final evaluation in person, over the phone, or by letter or e-mail. The student will always be involved in this.

The final evaluation may cover the following points:
- The student's commitment and motivation.
- Was the degree programme compatible with the tasks set for the student?
- Were there any knowledge gaps (methodological, statistical, subject related)?
- What was the quality of the product or products produced by the student?
- Could each of the student's products be used by the organization directly?
- What was the quality of the final report?
- Is the organization willing to continue working with students on placement?
- The student's competences. Is the student suitable for a position within the placement's discipline? If not, what other position is recommended?
- The student's learning objectives. Do the work environment and type of position appeal to the student? If not, what might be a more suitable environment?

Your degree programme or lecturer usually provides a standard final evaluation form.

7.3.2 Supervision by the Host Institution

Students are appointed practical supervisors at the placement site. Practical supervisors should meet at least these two criteria:
1. Their thinking and working level should correspond to that of the student's degree programme.
2. They should regularly be at or near the placement site or work near the student.

In addition, the practical supervisor should, of course, be willing and able to provide the student with regular feedback.

Agreements on the nature and extent of supervision by the practical supervisor are usually laid down in the placement contract (see Section 7.4). The interaction between the practical supervisor and the student is usually more intensive in observational placements than in project placements or research placements. It is sensible to structure the supervision by agreeing beforehand on the timing of feedback sessions, for example once a week at a fixed time. These moments can also be used to evaluate the student's functioning and, if necessary, to make adjustments.

7.4 Recording the Agreements in a Placement Contract

Many degree programmes provide a standard contract in which to lay down the placement agreements. Most of these contracts have been checked by in-house lawyers and are available in different languages. The contract must be signed by the practical supervisor, the supervising lecturer, the student, and sometimes also by the placement coordinator or other representative of your faculty or department.

Regular components that you may find in such a standard placement contract are as follows:

- the placement provider's name and address;
- the student's name, student number, and address;
- name of the degree programme and the supervising lecturer;
- duration of the placement and when it takes place plus the number of working hours per week;
- description of the placement assignment and other tasks;
- description of the supervision by the placement provider;
- description of the supervision by the faculty;
- the agreements with regard to the placement report, including deadlines;
- remuneration (if any);
- regulations regarding the placement's completion;
- regulations regarding copyright;
- regulations regarding insurance;
- supplementary provisions (if any);
- blank spaces for the signatures of the student, the lecturer, the practical supervisor, and possibly the placement coordinator or other representative of the faculty or department.

In principle, a placement contract does not qualify as a contract of employment, as it does not satisfy the conditions for performing work for a wage or salary. A placement remuneration is generally not considered to be a wage or salary, but an allowance. Only when the host institution is required to withhold tax from the remuneration can the placement be considered work. Please do verify this, because the regulations differ from country to country.

Placement activities are usually aimed at providing students with experience as part of their degree programme, which is why students on placement are regarded as students rather than employees (<www.internshipguide.elevenpub.com>). However, the relationship between students on placement and host institutions can often be considered a supervisory relationship. This means that placement providers have to observe the regulations regarding working conditions, working hours, and equal treatment with regard to the students on placement, as if they were the students' employers. In addition, special rules regarding working hours apply to underage students. If the Collective Labour Agreement (CAO) of the host institution contains special provisions regarding working hours, this does not, in principle, apply to students, although exceptions may be made. It is useful to find out which regulations apply to your situation.

The placement contract is usually a contract for a fixed term. At the end of the term, the contract terminates automatically by law. The contract may be terminated prematurely if one of the parties commits a breach of contract and therefore does not fulfil its obligations. This may occur, for instance, if the student misbehaves or if the host institution gives the student non-contracted work to do. The contract may also be terminated by mutual agreement. If the student sustains an injury at work, he or she may file a claim for damages against the placement provider. In cases like these, the allocation of the burden of proof is similar to that of a temporary worker claiming compensation from the user company.

In some cases, however, you may be given a contract of employment *in addition to* your placement contract. This is the case when the host institution actually legally employs you during your placement. You will then fall under the same regulations as regular employees. In that case, too, you will get a fixed-term contract of employment. At the end of that term, the contract ends by law. The employer will have to comply with all the regulations, including those for deducting payroll tax. This means that you will be entitled to a minimum wage. More information about this can be found on <www.internshipguide.elevenpub.com>.

Host institutions occasionally provide a placement contract of their own. Usually, it is no problem to use such a contract *in addition to* the one provided by the university. University contracts are primarily important for the student because, unlike contracts of the host institution, they cover the approval for the plans made by the student and placement provider. The university contract is also a guarantee that the placement, if it all goes according to plan, is awarded credits. You should read contracts carefully before signing them; sections on insurance and rights in contracts from placement providers are more than once in conflict with their university counterparts. Together with your lecturer, you can discuss such conflicting elements with your placement provider.

If you enter into a working relationship with the host institution, you may, besides a placement contract, also receive a letter of appointment. If you undertake a placement in a country other than your own, contact your university or the immigration office of that country to determine whether or not you need a work permit for the duration of your placement (see <www.internshipguide.elevenpub.com>).

7.4.1 Leave

It shouldn't be your first question when discussing the contract, but it is perfectly okay to ask whether you are allowed a day off during your placement. There are different ways in which leave for students on placement is arranged. Some students on placement get *no leave*, some get *unpaid leave*, some are entitled to the same holiday rights as regular employees, and some to a fixed number of leave days that applies to all students on placement. Example: a student is entitled to at least eight days of leave during a full-time placement of six months, to at least four days of leave during a full-time placement of three months, and to at least two days of leave per three months if it concerns a part-time placement.

You may have booked a holiday before you arranged your placement. If the holiday falls within the placement period, you should report this to the host institution well in advance. It may be a reason for them not to take you on after all, for instance if your holiday falls within a period when they really need you to be there. If you don't want to lose that particular placement opportunity, you might consider postponing your holiday instead.

If you want to take a day off, you should report this to your placement provider. There are particular days on which it is customary to get a day off, such as Easter, Christmas, and New Year's Day. This is not true for all placement providers, however. In the hotel and catering industry, for example, these are busy days on which your assistance is very much appreciated. Ask your employer when you have a day off or are allowed to take leave. Perhaps the best way to start this discussion is to ask about the organization's policy regarding leave for regular employees.

7.4.2   Sick Leave

Falling ill is usually not your own fault, and it is inconvenient for both you and your employer. It means that you have to take sick days. Ask your placement provider how this works and whom you need to report this to. If there were any important appointments or matters you had to take care of, you should first try to find a replacement yourself. Someone within the department may be able to fill in for you. Once you have recovered, you should again report to the relevant person.

If you think your illness prevents you from getting back to work soon, contact your employer. Illness should in all cases be reported to your supervising lecturer straightaway. He can tell you which university or school regulations are available to you in case of emergencies. Long-term illness often causes study delay, and this may have consequences for your student grant. Universities often provide financial aid in extraordinary circumstances (*e.g.* an emergency fund for students whose illness causes study delay), agreements regarding your student grant, or medical assistance and in-house bodies for care and aftercare. A student counsellor can help you with this.

7.4.3   Copyright

If any of the products of your placement is a text, film, or other copyrighted contribution, it would be wise to find out what the copyright regulations are. They are usually regulated by law. You can ask your placement coordinator or your university's legal department about them.

According to Dutch law, for instance, the copyright on the results of the placement report and/or thesis, including any appendices in the form of texts, DVDs, CDs, or MP3 files, is vested in the student on placement unless a written consent states otherwise. The host institution is entitled to use the placement's results for company purposes. The educational institution is entitled to use the placement's results for educational and research purposes.

7.4.4 Confidentiality

Your placement provider may request that a confidentiality clause be included in the contract. This can be the case for placements with, for example, the Ministry of Defence, multinationals competing in a highly competitive market, broadcasters, and organizations working with patients. If so requested by the company, the placement report should be treated confidentially, which means that no one but the lecturer is allowed to read it. Sometimes a student may write a cut-down version of the report in which only the personal views of the student are described and all information about the company is left out. This must, of course, be discussed with the lecturer in advance.

Standard placement contracts provided by universities contain no confidentiality clause because information obtained in educational settings must, in principle, be made available to staff and students of that educational institution. If your placement provider asks for it, then you can add such a clause. The contract often provides room for 'supplementary provisions'.

The confidentiality clause may be formulated in various ways. It should at least state that the student is required to maintain the confidentiality of what is entrusted to him in confidence during the placement period, and the same applies to any information that is available to him and that is or should be reasonably understood to be confidential. Placement providers are very strict about the observance of such agreements and will afterwards want to check whether the student did not fail to honour them.

7.4.5 Insurance

When undertaking a placement you also have to organize a few things in terms of insurance. Make sure you have third-party insurance, for instance. Check with your insurance company whether your third-party insurance covers your placement. In addition, your university may have taken out a *collective* liability insurance for students on placement. Finally, check with your placement provider if you fall under their liability insurance; this may be the case if the company offers you an employment contract for the length of the placement. Note that the third-party insurance of your university and host institution *supplement* your own third-party insurance. More on insurance for placements abroad can be found in Section 7.5.4.

In most cases, you will still be obliged to take out basic health insurance. If your placement requires you to move, remember to pass on your new address to your insurance company or companies. This is especially important for your contents insurance and, in case you are or will be a homeowner, your property insurance.

7.4.6   Financial Matters

Undertaking a placement is expensive. You are often required to move to another city (or country, but more on that later) and will sometimes need to resign from your part-time job. Some universities offer compensation towards some of the costs; others only provide grants in exceptional cases or emergencies. Organizations won't always shout this from the rooftops, so ask them about it.

> Leonie wants to do a placement with an NGO in Amsterdam. The aim of this NGO is to encourage, and increase the number of, women in top positions. They focus on developing countries. The NGO gladly accepts Leonie as a student on placement, and the lecturer of her degree programme in International Administrative Law gives his approval. Leonie has been a student for quite some time, which means she is no longer entitled to a student travel card. She will therefore have to buy a monthly ticket for the four months she will be travelling between her home in Beverwijk and the placement in Amsterdam. This will cost her €265 per month. She asks the placement coordinator whether she is entitled to a grant to compensate for these costs. The NGO has little money at its disposal because all its resources are geared towards the cause. The faculty contact person for placements suggests a fifty-fifty scheme: the faculty provides a €400 allowance, and the host institution has to support the remainder of the costs. Leonie is relieved and decides to accept the placement.

7.4.7   Housing

If you are going on placement in another municipality and are going to live there for a while, you must register with their Municipal Personal Records Database. Not being registered in the right city can have unpleasant consequences for your student grant.

7.5   Placement Abroad

Content-wise, a placement abroad usually doesn't differ all that much from a placement at home. You will have to make some additional arrangements, however. Step 5 discussed the important role that language and culture play in the preparation. You will also have to save more money. Additionally, you have to find out what insurance you need and whether you need a visa and/or vaccinations. Perhaps it is necessary that you report to the embassy of your home country because the situation in the country of your destination has been unstable at times. It will be harder to find a place to live from home, and it is advisable to ask for someone to pick you up from the airport. All these aspects mean that a placement abroad takes more time to prepare than a placement in your home country (for more information, go to <www.internshipguide.elevenpub.com>).

7.5.1   Financial Aspects of a Placement Abroad

A placement abroad is more costly than a placement in your own country. You can prepare yourself for the costs by drawing up a budget estimate. It would probably turn out that you have to save money first to avoid getting into too much debt.

The best way to keep the placement affordable is to search as long as you have to for a placement that comes with an attractive remuneration. If you have found a placement that, in your opinion, offers too low a remuneration, you can try to increase it through negotiation.

In addition to a remuneration, you may be eligible for a grant offered by your university. The European Commission provides a fund for placements within Europe, called *Erasmus Placements*, in which your university may be participating. Many universities provide their own grants for placements outside Europe. In addition, there are various grant directories that describe the various ways of finding a grant. Try to find out well in advance which grant your placement might qualify for, as there is often a limited amount of time to apply for one.

Sometimes it's useful to apply for a credit card. Perhaps there's a family member who can act as surety. You can authorize someone to represent you during your absence.

7.5.2   Living Abroad

If you undertake a placement abroad, there are several things you need to arrange in terms of housing. You have to let the local population registry, the bank, and the relevant student registration body know that you will be staying abroad.

You can sublet your room to avoid paying double rent. There are also websites geared to helping you arrange a room exchange. If there's a chance that you are not returning to the same city when your placement is over, it might be best to give up your room. The municipality should in all these cases be informed of your new address.

Quote from a student who undertook a placement abroad:

> I have seen, done, and experienced so much! First I was really worried whether I would be able to cope with it all, but everything turned out fine. I now have a much more balanced world view. I always thought my life in Scandinavia would be basically the same as my life in Canada. It turned out differently, but that only made it better. It was also great to realize that I possess the knowledge that was needed to make the placement a success. I now know that I want to go abroad after I graduate. I've actually known that for a long time, but now I also know that I *can*!

7.5.3 Visa

Make sure your passport is valid until *after* you return from your placement abroad. In addition, don't wait too long to figure out what other documents are needed for the country you are going to. The embassy or consulate of your home country can inform you about this. The visa application process can take considerable time and may involve extra costs.

Don't wait too long to figure out what documents and formalities need to be arranged before you leave. You won't need a work permit in the European Union, but you do need one outside it. Bear in mind that the process of applying for a visa or work permit for a non-European country may also involve a lot of time and effort.

147

7.5.4 Insurance Abroad

Insurance for placements abroad is divided into three types: third-party liability insurance, health insurance, and travel insurance.

Third-Party Insurance

A prerequisite for any placement is that you are insured for liability, either through your own insurance policy or that of your parents. It is important to find out whether this policy also covers your stay abroad. In addition, universities may have taken out a collective liability insurance for their students. This policy covers students on placement (or on study exchange) in case they cause damage to the host institution. In addition, your host institution may have taken out one or more insurance policies that also cover students on placement. The third-party insurance of your university and host institution always *supplements* your own liability insurance. Make sure that all insurance policies together sufficiently cover your liability and safety.

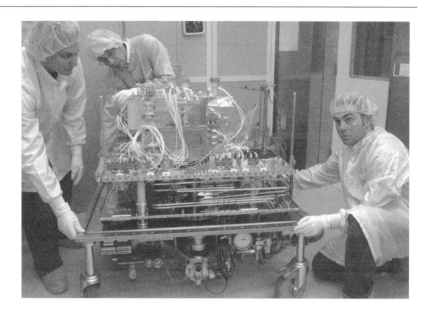

Health Insurance

Two things are important for your health insurance: your age and the duration of the placement abroad. You can find the most up-to-date information about health insurance on the website of the national organization for higher education of the country of your study (for links, go to <www.internshipguide.elevenpub.com>).

Medical expenses incurred abroad may not always be fully reimbursed. For full coverage you may therefore need *supplementary insurance*. Some private insurance companies offer supplementary insurance for persons obliged to take out basic insurance when travelling abroad. This could include coverage for medical expenses incurred abroad that are not covered by basic insurance, but it could also cover costs in case of accidents (including repatriation, among other things), liability, legal aid, etc.

Note that many insurance companies provide a supplementary health insurance that also offers medical coverage abroad. The repatriation expenses that are covered by this insurance usually only include repatriation for medical purposes. You are therefore advised to take out repatriation insurance to account for non-medical situations. We would suggest you check whether the insurance coverage for medical treatment abroad is valid for the entire length of your stay abroad, as they often come with a time limit of six or twelve months.

Basic insurance provides worldwide coverage, but you should ascertain whether the coverage suffices for the country you are going to. When reimbursing medical costs abroad, Dutch health insurance companies always base themselves on the *Dutch* prices for similar medical treatments. This may not be sufficient to cover the costs abroad. Before you go, check with your health insurance company which expenses are covered in the country you are going to. If setting a broken arm costs more in Argentina than in the Netherlands, will you be reimbursed for the amount you would pay in the Netherlands or the amount you actually have to pay the Argentinean hospital? Also, does the insurance policy for instance cover all malaria-related expenses in the developing country you are going to? Ask if you need a special international Health Insurance Card or any other form that entitles you to immediate necessary care abroad.

You might also want travel insurance. Some universities provide free travel insurance for their students. Information on this can be obtained from the International Office or Placement Office. If free travel insurance is not an option, they can probably refer you to insurance companies that allow you to take out pay-per-day insurance (instead of having to pay per month). Make sure that you're not paying double, for example for health care insurance. Your insurance company can help you with this.

7.5.5   Safety

If the security situation in a country deteriorates, travelling to a particular region – or any region, for that matter – may be discouraged. This is known as a 'negative travel advice'. Whether a negative travel advice has been issued can usually be found on the website of your country's Ministry of Foreign Affairs. The websites of the Australian Department of Foreign Affairs and the British Foreign Office also provide reliable advice. When you are dissuaded from travelling to a particular country, this does not always mean that the ministry concerned *forbids* it; it is a piece of advice that can either be taken or ignored.

Most universities advise against travelling to a country for which a negative travel advice has been issued. Under no circumstances will a university accept liability for damage or injury resulting from this advice being ignored. However, in some cases a placement may still be given the go-ahead, as, for instance, when the placement assignment and location are relevant to the degree programme's field, such as humanitarian aid. In addition, the student and family have to be okay with it. In such a case, the university is legally obliged not to withhold credits from the student after the placement has received approval. The student does have to be informed of the reasons for the negative travel advice, and has to sign an indemnification agreement once he does decide to go. More information on such an agreement can be found on <www.internshipguide.elevenpub.com>. Students who travel to a country despite a negative travel advice are usually not entitled to remuneration from their university. The collective liability insurance or travel insurance that the university normally provides are no longer in effect even if the student signs an indemnification agreement.

You are in all cases advised to report your trip to the embassy or consulate of your home country in the country of your destination. They need to know of any compatriots staying in the country at any time so that they can send SMS alerts or evacuate people in case of emergencies.

7.5.6 Medical Matters

When travelling to continents such as Africa and South America, you will likely need to get vaccinations or pills (*e.g.* to prevent malaria or Hepatitis B). You are advised to consult the municipal health service in good time about which vaccinations you need – these are often rather expensive. Before you leave, ask your dentist whether you need to take any precautions. If any health issues are expected, your doctor or dentist can give you the necessary medication as a precaution.

Sometimes students are required to submit a *health statement* to the placement provider. A GP, not necessarily your own, can provide you with such a statement. The costs of such a statement are not always covered by basic insurance. The tariffs are negotiable, so ask in advance what the costs will be. Needless to add, the health statement for placements abroad should be drafted in English.

7.5.7 Taxes

The Wages and Salaries Tax Act equates students on placement who receive a remuneration (allowance for expenses) with regular employees. Payroll tax is an advance on income tax. Students are advised to fill in a tax return of the tax authorities so that they can get back all or part of the tax they paid.

Students may get back quite a large amount of excess tax withheld, not only for paid placements, but also sometimes for part-time jobs. If you are doing both a part-time placement and a part-time job at the same time, you can usually get a tax refund for only one of them.

7.6 Progress

Students on placement will have little contact with their faculty during the placement. Perhaps the lecturer will grace the placement site with a visit, perhaps not.

It's important for the student to make proper arrangements with the lecturer beforehand regarding the time and manner of the interim evaluation as well as any interim reports he has to hand in (see Section 7.3.1).

7.6.1 Interim Report and Log

Writing interim reports or keeping a log during the placement makes it easier to write a placement report at the end. Even if the lecturer does not require you to, you will see that keeping notes of key matters is handy. Subjects may include:

- a short description of the work;
- anything about the placement that turned out better or worse than expected;
- things that caught you by surprise as an employee;
- your views on the things you learned in your degree programme from the perspective of your placement.

Additionally, the student can ask his practical supervisor to keep notes about him and to use these to write an assessment report. It is advisable to ask this at the very beginning, so that you can remind your supervisor of his or her promise at the end, if necessary (see Step 8).

7.6.2   Circumstances that Hinder the Progress of Your Placement

Some circumstances may hinder or even halt the placement's progress. If the cause of the obstruction lies with the placement contract (the duration, the assignment, the additional tasks, or the supervision), a solution has to be found in consultation with the lecturer and placement provider. Possible solutions are extending the placement, modifying the placement assignment, or providing an additional assignment. As the placement's project manager, the student has to make sure that all parties involved in the placement are informed of the modifications in time.

If the problems are caused by something else, there are special university bodies to help you deal with them, as in the following two cases, for example:

> Students with a performance disability are entitled to modified examinations and extra guidance by the study advisor. In addition, they often have several 'standard' facilities at their disposal. Students who require extra guidance owing to a performance disability, for example in finding a placement, can call on student counsellors.

> Students who encounter undesirable behaviour (*e.g.* sexual harassment, stalking) or unfair treatment on placement can call on the university's confidential advisor, if available.

There may be other situations that hinder the progress or completion of the placement. In all cases, the student has to report it to the lecturer and/or placement coordinator as soon as possible.

7.7   A Placement after Graduation

Perhaps you consider doing a placement after graduation. This may be the case if you didn't include a placement in your degree programme and want to gain experience, or if you want to get to know a field other than that of your previous placement. While such initiatives are indicated in this book as 'voluntary work' (because there are no credits involved), it is perfectly possible that your faculty supports your initiative for a post-Bachelor's or post-Master's placement. They may even have special contracts or provide you with a letter stating that you recently graduated. In addition, your university contact person can refer you to a careers advice centre that offers placement vacancies for recent graduates.

In all these cases, you should take into account additional costs. In most municipalities, you won't be able to claim benefit during your placement, because you are not available for work. Your placement won't yield a generous salary either; remunerations are usually no higher than €650 per month.

If you want to undertake a placement in a different European country after graduation, you might qualify for a Leonardo da Vinci grant. These grants from the European Commission are awarded through various university consortia. Addresses can be found at <www.internshipguide.elevenpub.com>.

Conclusion

Once you have found a placement, it must first be approved by your faculty. If you can't get it approved, you can still carry out the placement as a 'volunteer placement', which yields experience but no credits. Students usually gain approval for their placement through a placement plan, submitted to their lecturer. A placement plan also mentions whether it concerns a final-year project (*i.e.* a combination with a thesis or dissertation). If the lecturer gives you the green light, you can let the host institution know that the placement can go ahead. The host institution will also appoint a supervisor. The student can then, together with the supervisor and the lecturer, complete the *placement contract*. The student will also have to check his liability insurance, health insurance, and possibly his travel insurance. A placement abroad also requires the student to make preparations regarding finance, health, travel documents, permits, and safety. This entire procedure takes time and challenges the student to steer a middle course between the university's expectations (theoretical) and those of the host institution (practical). During the placement, it is advisable to keep a log with notes of the tasks you carry out and what you think of them. Halfway through the placement, the lecturer will carry out an interim evaluation with the student and the practical supervisor. In case there are certain factors that obstruct the placement's progress, the student should report them to both supervisors immediately. If there are no obstacles, the placement will be over before you know it. What happens then is discussed in Step 8.

153

Step 8   Rounding Off Your Placement

You have several options when your placement is over. Perhaps you're going to travel around for a bit in the country where you did your placement, or, more likely, return to your student life to graduate. If you undertook a placement abroad, you may experience 're-entry culture shock' upon returning home. Perhaps you are going to write your thesis and graduate. In that case, you will have to find a job once your placement is over; perhaps you can start working for your placement provider. Whatever you do, there will be a change in your daily routine. But before all that, there's still plenty to arrange.

Most importantly, your placement has to be evaluated by the practical supervisor at the host institution and by your lecturer after that. The assessment is often based on the placement report drawn up by the student. Based on this report and the practical supervisor's judgement, the lecturer will come to a final grade.

8.1   Placement Report

Placements are usually rounded off with a placement report with which the student provides both the placement provider and the supervising lecturer with an official account of the assignment and a critical assessment of the student's own performance. It can be in written form or in the form of a presentation, film, research paper, exhibition, or anything else that fits in with the placement and the degree programme.

Do not postpone writing your report until after the placement. Keep the deadline in mind. The report usually has to be submitted to the lecturer no later than three weeks after the placement. It is good practice to discuss the report with your practical supervisor before handing it in to the lecturer.

A placement report can include the following components:
- a cover (name, student number, address, telephone number, e-mail address, organization, name of practical supervisor, degree programme, and name of supervising lecturer);
- a title page;

- a short summary (optional);
- a preface (acknowledgements);
- a table of contents;
- an introduction (with answers to the questions: What was the placement assignment? Why this placement with this particular organization? What does this report cover?);
- a description of the placement (with answers to the questions: What was your learning objective, and what were the competences to be acquired? How would you describe the placement-providing organization? Which department did you work in? What did you do there?);
- an evaluation (with answers to the questions: What did you contribute to the organization? What knowledge and skills gained during your studies were you able to use? Did you achieve your learning objective? What competences did you acquire? Was your degree programme attuned to the practical field? And, possibly: Why did you undertake a placement? How did you find this placement? What was working like for you? How do you see your future on the labour market? What would you advise other students?);
- a conclusion (optional);
- references/notes;
- appendices (*e.g.* a research report or any other product you made during the placement).

Every degree programme has different guidelines governing the form and content of the placement report. These are the primary guidelines, of course. Guidelines may also differ according to placement type. When writing a report for a research placement, for instance, you have to include a chapter called 'Discussion' and state the problem definition in the introduction.

Faculties are legally obliged to archive placement reports for a specified period (*e.g.* five years). It is possible that, upon request, your faculty grants permission to enrolled students to consult these placement reports. Having a look at such sample reports may give you an even better idea of how to draw up your own. In some cases the host institution objects to this. If so, this is stated in the placement contract (under 'Supplementary provisions'). In that case, the report will be archived but made unavailable for inspection. Also, placement reports are usually scanned for fraud before they receive a grade.

8.2 Evaluation

The placement report forms the basis of the final evaluation (see Section 8.1). An assessment report or assessment form drawn up by the practical supervisor (see

Section 8.2.1) may also play a role. The final evaluation usually takes the form of a face-to-face interview and is led by the lecturer.

It's best if both placement supervisors and the student are present for the final evaluation. For placements that take place at a distance, the final evaluation may have to be carried out over the phone. Internet telephony and video conferencing make it possible for the three remote parties to meet simultaneously.

If it's not possible to arrange a meeting with both supervisors together, the parties have to speak to each other separately. An advantage of speaking with your supervisors separately is that you can rectify any mistakes you have made in your report on the basis of the practical supervisor's feedback (*e.g.* in your description of the organization). You will also get to learn first-hand what the placement provider thinks of your placement. Usually, the lecturer will then contact your practical supervisor to learn about his or her opinion of your placement. Once your lecturer has done that and has read the final version of your placement report, he or she will be ready to meet with you for the final interview.

8.2.1 *Final Evaluation by the Placement Provider*

It's best to ask your practical supervisor *before* the placement to draw up an assessment report at the end. This written evaluation addresses the competences you will have acquired by then and how you performed your tasks during the placement. The assessment report referred to here can be compared to the 'letter of recommendation' commonly used in the United States.

157

The idea behind an assessment report is that you can use it for future applications. A letter from your placement provider describing your performance at the workplace often tells a potential employer more about your work experience than your degree certificate or list of marks.

You can give your lecturer a copy of the assessment report so that he or she can take it into account when assessing your placement (see Section 8.2.2).

The *assessment report* by the practical supervisor may address:
- the execution of the placement assignment;
- the student's knowledge and skills at the start of the placement;
- the student's performance within the organization (with regard to the required competences, such as working independently, cooperation, communication skills, attitude, ingenuity, taking the initiative, productivity, efficiency, and flexibility);

- areas in which the student excels;
- areas in which the student could improve;
- the extent to which the learning outcomes mentioned in the placement plan have been achieved;
- the extent to which the placement report gives an accurate account;
- the placement supervision and any obstacles;
- an impression of the student's future career prospects, if possible.

As an alternative, many faculties provide an evaluation form for placement providers. This is usually a form on which the practical supervisor can assess some of the above-mentioned points as 'good', 'sufficient', or 'insufficient'. Perhaps this is what the lecturer needs to come to a final grade, but the report described above does seem to be more useful for your future.

8.2.2   Final Evaluation by the Lecturer

The final evaluation by the lecturer is usually carried out orally, in the presence of both the practical supervisor and the student. It's very unlikely that the three parties experienced the placement in the same way, so it's important to take this opportunity to discuss every experience and result step by step. All perspectives are represented so that differences in observation can, if necessary, immediately be adjusted by the three parties. Sometimes, an independent fourth party (in addition to the practical supervisor) is involved, too, such as an expert from the professional field in which the placement was carried out.

If the practical supervisor is unable to be present at the interview, it will take place between the student and the lecturer alone. In that case, the lecturer should have discussed the placement with the practical supervisor first, either by phone or (e-)mail. The student always has the right to know the outcome of this mutual evaluation.

In the final interview between the supervising lecturer and the practical supervisor (and, if possible, the student), the lecturer may discuss the following topics:
- A brief assessment of the *interim evaluation* (based on the lecturer's notes);
- An assessment of the second part of the placement (after the interim evaluation). Which tasks did the student carry out during the second part of the placement? What additional knowledge or skills did he or she apply? If any adjustments to the schedule or the assignment were made during the interim evaluation, have these changes been implemented successfully? (description by the practical supervisor);
- The practical supervisor's assessment of the competences acquired by the student, as set out in the placement plan;

- A discussion of the placement report;
- The practical supervisor's views regarding the student's suitability for a position within the discipline in which the placement was undertaken or possibly elsewhere. What are the student's qualities regarding this professional field? What could be improved?
- Any other observations, *e.g.* observations that are useful in order to improve the link between the degree programme and the professional field.

If the lecturer's meeting with the practical supervisor and the lecturer's meeting with the student take place separately, these topics will mostly be discussed in the latter.

Many degree programmes provide supervising lecturers with a standard evaluation form. A guide to assessment interviews with practical supervisors may also be available. Ask your faculty for more information.

8.2.3 *Final Evaluation by the Student*

After the final evaluation with your lecturer and practical supervisor, you may be asked to fill in an evaluation form yourself. The results of these evaluations provide the university with information about the quality of the content and organization of placements. You may also be asked about the possibilities of staying on at the organization once the placement is over. The university will use this information to improve placement regulations, placement content, and the information they provide to students.

8.3 Placement Assessment

The lecturer is responsible for the *assessment* and for awarding credits and a mark. Some degree programmes employ an external assessor or committee to determine part of the mark. The practical supervisor can provide input for the assessment on the basis of the student's achievements and the placement report. The practical supervisor can do this in the form of an assessment report, for example. Because the lecturer has not been closely involved in the placement, he or she is more or less forced to base the mark primarily on:

- the placement report with any accompanying end products, such as a recommendation, a plan, an exhibition, a festival, a conference, a book, an article, or a film;
- the interim evaluation, the final interview, and the practical supervisor's assessment report or evaluation form.

If the placement is the last component of the degree programme, the student often has to report this to the Student Administration Office immediately. They can then put the graduation procedure in motion.

8.4   Re-entry Culture Shock

Just as you can experience culture shock when you arrive in a foreign country, you can also experience culture shock upon returning home. This phenomenon is called *re-entry culture shock*. It may happen to you when you return from a journey (*e.g.* a placement) abroad, but may also happen when you return from a placement in your own country. The latter is an exception rather than the rule, so this section will primarily address the re-entry culture shock that students may experience after a placement abroad.

In 1981, the National Association for Foreign Student Affairs (NAFSA) conducted research into re-entry culture shock, and discovered that it may be just as intense and emotional as culture shock experienced abroad. After a phase of joy and euphoria, you may discover that your home environment has changed and may no longer be as nice and natural as you remember it. Your expectations of coming home may have been too optimistic. Because the culture of the country you visited affects your thoughts, values, and standards, you no longer feel completely at home in your country's culture.

> When Sandra enters the placement office to hand in the required papers after having returned from her placement in Uganda, the placement coordinator asks her if she suffered culture shock when she went there. 'No,' she says, 'but I did suffer culture shock when I got back in the Netherlands. My mother asked me if I wanted to go to the supermarket to buy groceries. She gave me *discount stickers* that I had to stick on the products. I really broke down a bit.'

Another problem you might encounter is that your environment shows little interest in your experiences and stories. Family and friends find it hard to picture themselves in your shoes. It is also possible that you changed your opinions and attitudes towards certain political and social issues. In addition, many students come home from a long trip with a greater sense of independence.

It is advisable to learn about culture shock and re-entry culture shock before you travel to a country in Asia, Africa, or Latin America. You will then at least be able to recognize the fears and problems you might experience. While not everyone suffers culture shock, it is good to be aware of the fears and problems you *could* encounter. If you want to know more, you can read about it in the lecturer's guide on <www.internshipguide.elevenpub.com>.

Naturally, not every student has to deal with fears and problems after returning home. On the contrary, a placement abroad often makes students interculturally competent. You develop skills for interpreting and establishing links between aspects of two different cultures, as well as social-interaction skills. You will probably develop a more open attitude and a heightened curiosity. In addition, you will increase your knowledge of social groups and the other culture, of intercultural differences, and of the interaction between persons and groups within those cultures …

8.5   Building on Acquired Competences

Many degree programmes pay attention to the student's acquired competences after they return from placement. Sometimes it is even initiated during the follow-up day halfway through the placement. Unfortunately, actually *building on* these competences often gets little attention because the placement is often scheduled near the end of the degree programme; also, it is hard to link follow-up courses to the vast variety of students' experiences.

161

The lack of connection between what you learned on placement and any courses you follow when you continue your studies may also cause feelings of alienation. Your motivation to graduate may increase but may also dwindle because of this. In any case, make sure that you make explicit what you think you know and can do. After all, the personal profile you drew up in Step 2 will have changed after the placement!

If you really want to do more with your placement than just graduate, do your utmost to share your experiences with others. Lecturers and study advisors will be thrilled if you offer to share your story, and fellow students will also want to learn from your approach. After all, even if you follow all eight steps in this book, your experience will be different from that of any other student on placement – and this, in particular, is what makes a placement such an enriching experience.

Conclusion

Once your placement is at an end, you will have to hand in a placement report to the lecturer for assessment. It is proper form to discuss your placement report with the practical supervisor – or someone else within the placement-providing

organization – first. Many degree programmes provide an assessment form for the placement provider, but you can also ask your practical supervisor to write an assessment report and to give your lecturer a copy. After returning from your placement, you may have a bit of a hangover: you are no longer an employee and colleague but have returned to being just a student. To prevent this from under-mining your motivation, you can share your placement experiences with as many people as possible. You can also share them on <www.internshipguide.elevenpub. com>!

Bibliography

Abma, Albert-Jan, Chris Coolsma, Elise Kamphuis, Mila Smrkovsky, and Esther Haag. 'Stage Nieuwe stijl in het Universitair Onderwijs'. *Onderwijsinnovatie* 10.3 (2008): 16, 27-29.

Boland, Cathalijne (ed.). *Het Boek WERK: Alles over Werk en Loopbaan.* Amsterdam: Balans/Intermediair, 2010.

Bolles, Richard N. *Welke Kleur Heeft Jouw Parachute? Een Praktisch Handboek voor Werkzoekers en Carrièreplanners.* Amsterdam: Nieuwezijds, 2005.

Bolte, Geerhard. *Functie: Sollicitant: Solliciteren Nieuwe Stijl.* Utrecht: Spectrum, 2003. Print. Volkskrant Banen.

Dam, Geertje. 'Corporate Identity Model'. 2009.

Foust, Stephen. *Learning across Cultures: International Communication and International Education Exchange.* N.W. Washington, DC: National Association for Foreign Student Affairs, 1981.

Gonzalez, Julia, and Robert Wagenaar. *Tuning Educational Structures in Europe. Universities' Contribution to the Bologna Process. An Introduction.* 2nd ed. Bilbao: U o Deusto, 2008.

Haag, Esther, and Jeanne Dirven. 2008. *Schrijven in Stappen: Handboek voor de Verslaglegging van Literatuuronderzoek.* The Hague: Lemma, 2008.

Hofstede, Geert, and Gert Jan Hofstede. *Cultures and Organizations: Software of the Mind. Intercultural Cooperation and Its Importance for Survival.* 2nd ed. New York: McGraw-Hill, 2005.

Lampe, Tecla T.M., Piet J.M. Hendriks & Gerard J.J.M. Straetmans. 2009. Zijn studenten beroepsbekwaam na hun praktijkstage? In: *Onderwijsinnovatie* 10.4 (2009): 11-13.

Sanders, Geert, and Bram Nuijen. *Bedrijfscultuur: Diagnose en Beïnvloeding.* Assen: Van Gorcum, 1992.

Van Eeden, Rob. *Netwerken Werkt: Op Weg naar de Baan Die Je Wilt.* Utrecht: Spectrum, 2004. Volkskrant Banen.

Villa Sánchez, Aurelio, and Manuel Poblete Ruiz (eds.). *Competence-based Learning: A Proposal for the Assessment of Generic Competences.* Bilbao: U o Deusto, 2008.

Index